DECOLONIZING CULTURE

ESSAYS ON THE INTERSECTION OF ART AND POLITICS

ANURADHA **VIKRAM**

This collection is dedicated to the memory of two curators
and friends whose thinking has informed my writing:

Coosje van Bruggen (1942–2009) and
Leigh Markopoulos (1968–2017)

TABLE OF
CONTENTS

Foreword

This volume is a collection of seventeen essays written by Anuradha Vikram for #Hashtags, a column on *Daily Serving*, between July 2013 and May 2017. #Hashtags originated as a series in August 2011, under the direction of then-managing editor Julie Henson. At the time, *Daily Serving* was rapidly expanding, both in the scope of its audience and the range of its coverage. Henson conceived of #Hashtags in order to make clear the organization's artist-centric stance on the art world's social, cultural, and political spheres of influence, and to reflect the viral nature of art-world issues. The column's tag line makes clear its intended mission: *a series exploring the intersection of art, social issues, and global politics.* Although these concerns were already appearing in the reviews and essays published on *Daily Serving* since its inception in 2006, it was critical to specify an intentional space for them—a place for an explicit conversation rather than afterthoughts. In the beginning, the column served as a repository for any socially and politically minded essay. The main contributors were Danielle Sommer and Matthew Harrison Tedford, with guest appearances by Rob Marks, Robert Gomez, and others. These articles set the tone for what would become one of the longest running columns on *Daily Serving* and initiated an invaluable critical space for analyzing the larger social realities of the art world in our present time.

When I was hired to be the managing editor of *Daily Serving* in May 2013, one of my first tasks was to seek a new writer for #Hashtags. I wanted to see what would happen if, instead of using the column as an ideological receptacle for many authors, we created space for a singular voice who could provide a continuous first-person perspective, succinctly describe and problematize the issues, suggest solutions and remedies, and call out antagonists. I wanted a tireless observer with a keen perception of the subtle dynamics of social hierarchies, who could speak truth to power, and advocate for artists— especially those artists from or working within marginalized populations. Knowledgeable, thoughtful, and critically engaged with the social and political aspects of contemporary artistic production, Anuradha Vikram was my first choice. At that time, Anu was teaching seminars on critical theory and culture at UC Berkeley and San Jose State, contributing to journals such as *Leonardo* and *Afterimage*, and had been curating exhibitions for nearly a decade. Since meeting Anu, I had been fortunate enough to engage with her in numerous conversations about intentionally creating space for arts workers of color. I felt as though the #Hashtags column was waiting for her to step into the role.

From the beginning, it seemed both essential and entirely logical that Anu should have unrestricted agency in determining the focus and content of each column. This non-prescriptive approach meant that Anu would have the freedom to tackle whatever she wanted. And she aimed to tackle a lot—subjects as broad as the terminology used throughout the global art community and as specific as the economic forces at work within a single neighborhood in Los Angeles.

Over the past four years, Anu has written essays investigating a wide range of issues that affect the arts, both visibly (race, representation, gentrification) and invisibly (market forces, class), using exhibitions as jumping-off points to address broader issues. As responses to specific artworks and events, the essays are written ex post facto, but they are forward-thinking in that they insist on—and often trace a path to—a more equitable future. Though Anu responds to events that are also covered by other writers, her uniquely pointed analysis reveals aspects of culture whose complexity goes unacknowledged in many other arts essays. For instance, in "Sweet and Low," she describes the nuanced interaction between gentrification, public art, and private funding: "The appetites of development, whether represented by Brooklyn condominium developers, Russian oligarchs, or the Israeli Army, trump human values despite the professed commitment to socially engaged artistic practices." If there is a subtle point to be made, Anu rarely misses it; in "The Painting," she takes on the controversy surrounding Dana Schutz's racially charged painting of Emmett Till and locates the exact moment in which Whitney Biennial curators Christopher Y. Lew and Mia Locks blundered: "[…] by neglecting to recognize that a white artist's engagement must be with the racial imaginary of whiteness in order to matter." Anu is never afraid to punch upward: in "Toward the Black Museum," she observes, "[the Contemporary Art Museum St. Louis] chose to claim a space for Blackness and then fill it with white guilt."

Through these seventeen essays, Anu shows us that art and culture can never be separated from the social, political, and economic circumstances under which they are produced and exhibited. Anu's email reply to my May 2013 offer to be the new #Hashtags columnist began, "I would absolutely love to do this. Thank you for thinking of me!" But it is I who must thank Anu, for thinking through the many crucial and intricate issues contained here.

Bean Gilsdorf
Editor in Chief, *Daily Serving*
San Francisco, July 2017

Can Art Persist?

At the time of this writing (June 2017), Dakota elders in the Minneapolis region are considering the ritual burning of elements taken from *Scaffold*, Sam Durant's large-scale public sculpture, now dismantled and removed from its site in the Walker Art Center Sculpture Garden. Durant, a white, male-identified artist whose work centers on the monument as a site of reckoning with a violent historical past, has reportedly agreed to the sculpture's destruction at the request of tribal leaders. *Scaffold* was acquired by the Walker for its permanent collection as one of seventeen new sculptures added to the public sculpture park; it references the hanging of thirty-eight Dakota tribesmen in 1862 in nearby Mankato, Minnesota. The sculpture was perceived by Native American community members as a hurtful reminder of colonial aggression, manifesting through both state-sponsored acts of killing and the ongoing soft-power antagonism of exclusion directed at Native artists and cultural producers. Protest signs at the site proclaimed the structure "Not Art."

Reaction to *Scaffold*'s destruction has been varied. Many artists and culture workers see the outcry as an act of censorship and the burning as a dangerous precedent. A work of art already in the public realm should be preserved, goes their argument, irrespective of its cultural interpretation by the public. Once an artwork leaves the studio, the artist's prerogative to destroy it conflicts with the imperative of provenance, in which an artwork is an artwork forever. In this way, the controversy over *Scaffold* is misunderstood to be in line with the objections to Dana Schutz's *Open Casket* at the Whitney (discussed elsewhere in this volume). The problem is thought to be that the wrong person—a white person—is addressing a history of white-inflicted trauma on non-white communities from the perspective of the victims, a vantage point that they cannot understand.

In the case of *Scaffold*, though, it's not about who has the right to speak and to be heard. It's about who has the right to resources, or to simply to take up space. In the face of the ongoing violence at Standing Rock, it is not hard to imagine why the Durant sculpture felt like salt in a fresh wound. It is more difficult to understand why none of the highly qualified art professionals involved with the work's purchase considered that placing a racially charged hanging platform in the middle of a landscape of pleasure, presented for the enjoyment of predominantly white visitors, might be a provocation.

In the late 1960s, the focus of art moved from physical objects to a network of associations, systems, signs, and concepts, and a subtle but pervasive inequality took hold. Political art became a way to represent people of color and those historically disenfranchised within the discourse of culture, but without making the mechanisms of the culture industry accessible to them in any structural way. Meanwhile, cultural expressions stemming from existing non-Western cultural traditions were marginalized by the shift to conceptual and time-based "contemporary art," a term that should be understood to represent a specific stylistic movement like "Modernism," rather than a catch-all for art made during a certain time period. Today, the art market consumes images rapaciously, including those that engage difficult social questions, mainly unconcerned by any critical or culturally specific content they might hold. Museums in the United States are hamstrung by an art market that serves speculators above the public interest, a tax code that relegates curators to personal shoppers cajoling trustees to make promised gifts, and an ongoing real-estate fetish that turns directors into developers instead of caretakers. The public, while important to bring in, is too often low on the list of constituencies to understand and serve.

Politically radical conceptual art, though it celebrates the working class, still presumes a high level of education and visual sophistication on the part of the viewer. Minimalist art, despite its economy of gesture, commands an enormous amount of space. When critics call this work "white art" (as the graffiti on a gallery door in Boyle Heights, Los Angeles, declared late last year), what they mean is that this kind of art is deliberately inaccessible to people who don't have access to means, and haven't been groomed for it by passage through white-dominated institutions. It doesn't mean that only white artists can make this work, or even that artists of color cannot represent their interests through these practices. It does mean that those artists of color who work in this way can expect that their work will be seen and experienced primarily by white audiences and reviewed by white critics.

If nothing else, I would like this volume to stand as a rejoinder against the expectation that the only qualified audiences for contemporary art are white audiences, and that the only qualified makers are artists trained in a system built to serve white cultural dominance. This is too often assumed by both art elites and populists. Artists of color who refuse to conform to externally dictated characteristics of their racial and national identities and white artists who accept the responsibility to engage in deep, research-based acts of self-critique deserve critical readings that reflect the multifaceted understandings they bring to these topics. When the political intention of the work is diluted by structural contradictions in its financing, I believe it is in the interest of the artist, the institution, and the public for critics to address those conflicts frankly and fairly, in detail. It has been my privilege to learn from each of the artists and curators whose work I cover in these texts. Whether or not I agree with their choices, I appreciate the vulnerability implicit in the act of putting one's ideas on display for another—the critic—to pick apart and second-guess. Thank you for giving me such rich material to work from.

Anuradha Vikram
Los Angeles, June 2017

I.

BEING THERE

The Political Biennale

The 56th Venice Biennale, *All the World's Futures* (2015), has been hailed as the "political" Biennale by both its curator, Okwui Enwezor, and the international art press. That designation has come in for significant criticism from some who feel that contemporary art either cannot or should not address political concerns, given the commodity status of art objects within a capitalist framework. Supported by a consortium of state, corporate, and individual interests, none of which can be assumed to represent progressive values or the rights of the disenfranchised, the Biennale in fact functions as a bazaar in which established and emerging national interests jockey for influence, applying both "soft" cultural power and "hard" economic power. How, then, to reconcile the Biennale's nature with the "deeply reflective, deeply political"[1] objectives that Enwezor has laid out?

Enwezor declares that his exhibition, the centerpiece of an international festival presenting pavilions from eighty-seven nations,[2] addresses "the ruptures that surround and abound around every corner of the global landscape today." He draws legitimacy for his project's geopolitical framework from history, describing how "[o]ne hundred years after the first shots of the First World War were fired in 1914, and seventy-five years after the beginning of the Second World War in 1939, the global landscape again lies shattered and in disarray, scarred by violent turmoil, panicked by specters of economic crisis and viral pandemonium, secessionist politics, and a humanitarian catastrophe on the high seas, deserts, and borderlands, as immigrants, refugees, and desperate peoples seek refuge in seemingly calmer and prosperous lands."[3]

Critics such as *artnet*'s JJ Charlesworth have accused Enwezor of trivializing serious global crises by engaging them through the lens of art. "Underneath all the political posturing," Charlesworth objects, "what it really represents is a bad case of disavowal—of not wanting to admit that you're part of a system that is the problem, not the solution."[4] Readers of #Hashtags will know that the art world's complicity in oligarchic and hegemonic systems is one of my favorite subjects. Nonetheless, I find Charlesworth's declaration that "the real point for all these countries and non-countries is to be part of the new machinery of the global economic world order"[5] to be factually accurate but ethically disingenuous. This may be the motivation for government support of national pavilions, but it is not the motivation for artists who choose to engage political and historical narratives in their work.

Charlesworth dismisses the point that for those born outside the halls of influence established in the colonial era, the only way to attain visibility as a representative of the global under-class is to engage with the machinery of power. Yet he and other art critics are themselves complicit in a system that refuses to give attention to artists who exist outside of it, whether by choice or by exclusion. If "the art itself changes absolutely nothing," as Charlesworth claims in his piece, this is not because political art is inherently futile, but because post-colonial reality is one of sublimated, rather than reformed, structural oppressions. No longer can cultural or political exclusion be articulated purely in terms of race or national origin; rather, the same structures of exclusion are applied across geopolitical boundaries on the basis of class, educational access, and entrenched tribalism. This is as true in the art world as anywhere else.

Despite the proliferation of international art festivals and fairs, the center of cultural discourse is still located in the Western hemisphere, as demonstrated by the clamor of developing nations asking to be included in the Venice Biennale. Enwezor himself was not anointed as an elite curator through his organizing of the 2nd Johannesburg Biennale, in 1997, but through his appointment as curator of Documenta 11, in 2002. No doubt, his high profile has been sustained by his adherence to the protocols of art-world exclusivity—obtuse academic speak, globetrotting, glitzy compadres. No curator who has attained the level of visibility necessary to be appointed to curate at Venice is free of such baggage. The difference here is that Enwezor is Black and African, and the white critical establishment is quick to position him as a representative of communities they have worked hard to exclude and to suggest he is personally responsible for correcting wrongs that cultural insiders are permitted to ignore.

What, then, of the politics at play within the exhibition? Modes of engagement run the gamut, from aesthetic gestures like Adel Abdessemed's bouquets of inverted knives and Melvin Edwards's assemblages made from tools and shackles, to more prescriptive manifestations like Gulf Labor Coalition's enormous banner outlining labor abuses at global museum construction sites on Saadiyat Island in the United Arab Emirates.[6] The strongest works are those that negotiate the poles of aestheticism and political expression, such as the collection of anti-Putin protest garments assembled by Russian artist GLUKLYA (Natalia Pershina-Yakimanskaya), of collective Chto Delat?, which fluctuate between social operation in the sphere of protest and aesthetic function in the space of installation. Arguably the most powerful work in this massive exhibition is the film *Vertigo Sea* (2015), by Ghanaian-British filmmaker John Akomfrah, a meditation on the ocean's many uses, from ecology to migration to commerce, that masterfully dances between breathtaking beauty and equally gasp-inducing horror.

Enwezor is correct when he suggests that "[e]verywhere one turns, new crisis, uncertainty, and deepening insecurity across all regions of the world seem to leap into view."[7] Despite this, beauty expresses itself through sound and form throughout this exhibition. It's evident in the bright color sprays of Katharina Grosse's *Untitled Trumpet* (2015) and the haunting harmonies of Lili Reynaud Dewar's *My Epidemic (Small Bad Blood Opera)* (2015). Rather than get hung up on Isaac Julien's recitations of *Das Kapital* (which even Enwezor admits is "a book that nobody has read and yet everyone hates or quotes from"),[8] a more engaged viewer might see these readings as part of a larger program of live performance that periodically animates the installation.[9] This is true in David Adjaye's massive red "Arena" and throughout both exhibition venues, with musical compositions arranged by artists including Charles Gaines,

#CAPITAL #LABOR #PROTEST #GLOBALIZATION #ACCESS #POWER #INSTITUTIONS #NATIONALISM

Jason Moran and Alicia Hall Moran, Jeremy Deller, and Jennifer Allora and Guillermo Calzadilla.

For some, the only question to be answered by political art remains, does it change anything? This is not my chief concern, as I staunchly support the right of art to serve no greater purpose than provoking discourse and thought within its viewership. However, let us consider what efficacy might be sought from projects like Vik Muniz's *Lampedusa* (2015), a "paper" boat, adorned with headlines from Italian news coverage of a 2013 tragedy in which hundreds of Libyan migrants drowned off the coast of Italy, that traverses Venice's canals. Will Muniz prevent another migrant tragedy through his artwork? Unlikely. Will his work promote awareness of this abysmal tragedy to an audience of oligarchs and tourists vacationing along the Canal? Questionable. Does this work, therefore, trivialize the incident?[10] Only if one believes that artistic commentary is implicitly less serious than journalism or policy, frameworks that have failed to provoke sufficient outrage at the conditions that lead to recurring tragedies of this kind. The expectation that art, with far fewer resources than government,[11] should accomplish a greater result or abandon social engagement altogether serves as a backhanded means of silencing artists whose work strays from upbeat, market-friendly narratives.

Meanwhile, invited artist Gulf Labor Coalition made its contribution an actual protest, staging an action on May 8, 2015, that shut down the Peggy Guggenheim Collection and forced the museum's director Richard Armstrong to agree to a meeting about labor abuses at the Guggenheim Abu Dhabi's Saadiyat Island construction site. Given that Gulf Labor activists such as Walid Raad and Ashok Sukumaran have recently been refused entry to the United Arab Emirates to speak about labor issues, present their art, and document conditions under which migrant laborers live, the international territory of the Biennale becomes a fruitful alternative site for their interventions.[12] When the attention of the world's powerful is focused on a single location, it is not pointless or hypocritical to raise issues of inequality and marginalization. Rather, it is necessary. To reject the potential of such gestures is to justify the inaction of the status quo.

1   Higgins, "Das Kapital at the Arsenale," *Guardian*.

2   Two pavilions, Kenya and Costa Rica, were withdrawn shortly before opening, illustrating the contradictions of the Biennale's geopolitics. Kenya withdrew following controversy over its inclusion of Italian and Chinese artists at the expense of Kenyans, while Costa Rica withdrew when artists protested its pay-to-play model. In both cases, the state's desire to benefit from the Biennale's visibility was shown to be incommensurate with that state's support for its artists.

3   Enwezor, "All the World's Futures."

4   Charlesworth, "Playing Politics," *artnet*.

5   Ibid.

6   Founded in 2011, Gulf Labor Coalition is a coalition of "international artists working to ensure that migrant worker rights are protected during the construction of museums on Saadiyat Island in Abu Dhabi." Its core members include Haig Aivazian, Ayreen Anastas, Doug Ashford, Doris Bittar, Sam Durant, Rene Gabri, Hans Haacke, Guy Mannes-Abbott, Michael Rakowitz, Walid Raad, Andrew Ross, Gregory Sholette, Ashok Sukumaran, Shaina Anand, Mariam Ghani, Naeem Mohaiemen, Tania Bruguera, Rene Gabri, Nitasha Dhillon, Amin Husain, Paula Chakravartty, and Noah Fischer. See: https://gulflabor.org/.

7   Enwezor, "All the World's Futures."

8   Higgins, "Das Kapital at the Arsenale."

9   A sharper critique of the live art program would address the hierarchical and remote, theatrical nature of the performances in an era when interactivity and participation hold sway.

10   For more discussion of Muniz's piece, see: Muñoz-Alonso, "Why Does Vik Muniz's Giant Paper Boat for the Venice Biennale Trivialize Europe's Migrant Crisis?," *artnet*.

11   Despite the enormous sums of money at play in the art world, working artists still receive very little investment. Numerous participants in the Biennale have described to me the financial burden they personally took on to participate.

12   For Raad's statement on the experience, see: Vartanian, "Artist Walid Raad Denied Entry into UAE, Becoming Third Gulf Labor Member Turned Away," *Hyperallergic*.

Whose Museum Is It Anyway?

Two major New York exhibitions this winter have raised the question of access to contemporary art and museums in important and divergent ways. *Radical Presence: Black Performance in Contemporary Art* (2013–2014) at the Studio Museum in Harlem continues reframing the historical narrative to include African Americans, as begun in the exhibition's Part 1, at New York University's Grey Art Gallery. Mike Kelley's sprawling retrospective at MoMA PS1 (2013–2014; originating at Stedelijk Museum, Amsterdam, and traveling to the Museum of Contemporary Art, Los Angeles) similarly engages questions of identity and inclusion within the context of a white American artist's experience of the world.

In my review of *Radical Presence*, published on *Daily Serving*, I identified the absence of a cohesive vision of "Black performance" that diverged substantively from the larger framework of post-conceptual performance art in terms of form rather than culturally specific content.[1] This line of inquiry was inspired by the exhibition's wall text, which asserted that "Black performance has generally been associated with music, theater, dance, and popular culture," and proposed to re-situate these practices within the visual-arts genre of performance. Why, I wondered, did curator Valerie Cassel Oliver not frame the show more forcefully as a reconsideration of performance-art histories that have tended to omit the contributions of Black artists? Why did she locate the radical shift within the Black community's traditional framework for performance rather than use it to lay claim to the white-dominated narratives of conceptual and action-based art? At the time, it seemed unlikely to me that a significant number of Black visitors unfamiliar with late twentieth-century performance art would be attending the exhibition in lower Manhattan. I assumed that audiences of any color would be contemporary art audiences experienced in the conventions of live art. Having now experienced the second part of the exhibition at the Studio Museum, I perceive that the question of what makes "Black performance" Black has taken a backseat to the question of what has historically rendered modern and contemporary art venues "white," and that Cassel Oliver may have been trying to establish a point of entry to those who could be most likely to exclude themselves from the intended audience for her show.

Author David Osa Amadasun tackled this question recently in an article titled "'Black People Don't Go to Galleries'—The Reproduction of Taste and Cultural Value."[2] Amadasun describes how every aspect of the museum-going experience, from institutional architecture to the politics expressed by exhibiting artists, to education programs aimed at audience diversification, is framed in such a way that visitors of color see themselves positioned on the outside. Some of this may be internalized micro-aggression, such that people of color imagine themselves to be out of place in these spaces of culture before any move has been made to actively exclude them. Much of it is structural, maintained by inherited systems of cultural display that originate in imperialist subjugation of non-Western peoples by Europeans and the simultaneous removal and exaltation of their cultural production.

Given this context, Cassel Oliver likely chose to frame the history of Black performance in a way that would be familiar to Black audiences rather than contemporary art audiences. However, by doing so she may be serving audiences at the expense of artists who deserve to be viewed as central to the historical narrative of live art from which they have been excluded due to their racial backgrounds. Also, while the general audience of color that Cassel Oliver appears to address is present at the Studio Museum, which is located in a walking and shopping district in a majority-minority neighborhood, it is less in evidence at Grey Art Gallery, a downtown university gallery that draws students, tourists, and art patrons. The decision to split this exhibition into two separate venues for its New York run complicates and confuses the message as well as the form of the show, which suffers as a result.

That said, the second half of *Radical Presence* is a darker and more compelling show than the first. Works such as Wayne Hodge's *Negerkuss (Variation #1)* (2011), Tameka Norris's untitled performance (2013) involving painting the walls with her slit tongue and lemon juice, and Dave McKenzie's *Fight Club*-inspired video *Edward and Me* (2000) all articulate the anger, pain, and internal conflict that African Americans continually experience despite the collective fiction of a "post-racial" paradigm. William Pope.L, whose work at Grey Art Gallery I called "the clear front-runner for the most confrontational expression of the Black experience,"[3] shows a wholly different side of his practice at the Studio Museum, riffing on the role of the artist as academic in *Another Kind of Love: John Cage's Silence, by Hand* (2013). In this work paying homage to Cage's famously silent composition, *4'33"* (1952), Pope.L stakes his claim to the modernist legacy of live art that Cassel Oliver's curatorial narrative skirts.

Brown bodies also factor in the Studio Museum show in works by Papo Colo, Girl (Chitra Ganesh and Simone Leigh), and Xaviera Simmons. Colo's Puerto Rican heritage is African, Hispanic, and Indigenous, as are the politics of his work. Girl is a collaboration between a South Asian and an African American artist that explores the societal baggage borne by women of color who are frequently excluded from both feminist and racial-justice conversations. Simmons turns the tables on cultural tourism, transforming herself from a Western tourist on a Sri Lankan train to a member of an impromptu community of locals by responding constructively to their discomfort with her difference.

An intersectional view of difference would suggest that locating it in race alone discounts equally significant factors of class, gender, education, sexual identification, and labor. Taking this view, it is possible to see MOMA PS1's monumental survey of Kelley's work as another meditation on difference and exclusion in the context of institutions. The setting of this show at a former public school could not be more apt, given that school is the primary site of trauma that Kelley revisits compulsively throughout his vast body of work. That trauma is paralleled in the artist's experiences as a working-class hero in the spaces of high culture. Kelley's art reads as a form of white-male identity politics in that he applies methodologies of re-creating social traumas and exaggerating those aspects of his persona that are perceived as most perverse and threatening by polite society and that characterize the work of his most confrontational peers among artists of color. Like the artists in *Radical Presence*, Kelley is primarily an artist working in performance, and like them, he disseminates embodied actions into sculpture, assemblage, painting, and installation.

Numerous works treat the architectures of schools as spaces of indoctrination and abuse. Kelley's *Day Is Done* (2005–2006), a large-scale, multi-channel video installation, restages photographs of extracurricular activities from a found high school yearbook as performances of repressed trauma and occasionally of liberation. Each video is sited within a fabricated architecture, so as to impregnate built space with the social oppression it carries forth implicitly. Other works map the rooms of various schools, including Wayne High near Detroit, from which Kelley graduated, and CalArts, in Valencia, where he taught, according to their psychological import. While the works are often funny and occasionally sweet, it is clear that Kelley did not retain positive associations from his time in educational spaces.

He made his feelings of discomfort with the structural classism of art museums equally clear in a large installation, *From My Institution to Yours* (1987), now installed in PS1's basement. Juxtaposing crude cartoony illustrations with wary texts, Kelley constructed a roped-off space replete with red carpet. This reified architecture is connected by a red ribbon to the depths of the museum, leading viewers to confront the barriers erected between themselves and the institution's administrative staff. A large battering ram lies in front of a door marked "Employees Only," dents and rust visible on the door's surface. When this work was installed at Los Angeles County Museum of Art in 1987, Kelley exhorted viewers to "Climb over the rampart. Batter down the door. Step across the line that separates brother and sister from brother and sister."[4] At PS1, that line of separation was enforced by one of dozens of African American museum guards enlisted to defend a hierarchy that places them firmly at the bottom. I asked the guard which person had been given the job of professionally battering the door. Was it him? He laughed, "I'd lose my job." More likely it was members of the preparatory staff, freelance laborers who are mostly artists and mostly working class, and whose symbolic battering represents a gesture of resistance thoroughly neutered by structures of exclusion.

The Kelley show is a Freudian funhouse, rife with meditations on failure, self-loathing, cruelty, and rage. His years in Los Angeles are made most tangible by his explorations of Hollywood's dual nature as a dream factory and a sleazy flesh trade. His lifelong struggle with depression and his equally characteristic popular-culture obsessions come together in the *Kandor* works, which represent the novel union of Superman and Sylvia Plath. There is enough here to fill volumes with interpretation, and each reading of Kelley's oeuvre says as much about the analyst as about the artist. The exhibition is a memorial as well as a retrospective, and the pain of curator Ann Goldstein (former Stedelijk director, longtime Museum of Contemporary Art, Los Angeles, curator and Kelley champion) over the artist's 2012 suicide is palpable in the way the whole affair often feels like an undifferentiated display of the contents of a beloved but troubled uncle's estate. The lack of distance leads to some questionable curatorial choices, but ultimately, that raw emotional core brings the show to life. Mike Kelley's work continues to push buttons precisely because, for all his success, he never forgot who he was or who the art markets or institutions were there to serve. Posthumously, his work continues to function as a lifeline for those of us who are compelled to participate in the systems of contemporary art even though they repeatedly push us away, knock us over, and kick us when we're down.

#INTERSECTIONALITY #PERFORMANCE #CLASS #RACE #INSTITUTIONS #ACCESS

1   Vikram, "Radical Presence," *Daily Serving.*

2   Amadasun, "'Black People Don't Go to Galleries'—The Reproduction of Taste and Cultural Value," *Media Diversified.*

3   Vikram, "Radical Presence."

4   Gonzalez, "Step Across the Line: Mike Kelley, 1954–2012," *Unframed.*

The Ethnicity Exhibition

Since the Civil Rights Era, it has become commonplace for marginalized ethnic communities to instate their own institutions of sociological and cultural study such as university Ethnic Studies departments and museums like Brooklyn's Museum of Contemporary African Diaspora Arts. In the face of extreme prejudice and exclusion from the discourses of history and art, many have felt the necessity and urgency of race-focused research. Nonetheless, in a global art market such as we have today, the existence of numerous star artists of color has prompted some to ask whether the race-based exhibition has run its course as a format for relevant artistic exchange. Recently, Adrian Piper's request to withdraw her work from the exhibition *Radical Presence: Black Performance in Contemporary Art* (2013–2014) at New York University's Grey Art Gallery stirred up debate around ethnocentric exhibitions once more.

Piper's request that documentation of her work *The Mythic Being* (1973) be pulled from the exhibition was executed with high drama, coming after the show had opened and the work was already on view. The timing of her withdrawal is inexplicable considering the work had been included in the full run of *Radical Presence* at its originating institution, Contemporary Arts Museum Houston. Her request read, in part: "Perhaps a more effective way to 'celebrate [me], [my] work and [my] contributions to not only the art world at large, but also a generation of black artists working in performance,' might be to curate multi-ethnic exhibitions that give American audiences the rare opportunity to measure directly the groundbreaking achievements of African American artists against those of their peers in 'the art world at large.'"[1] For her part, curator Valerie Cassel Oliver has said that *Radical Presence* intends to "resist reductive conclusions about blackness"[2] and to present a version of performance in Black history that transcends traditional categories of music, dance, and storytelling. Seeking to define African American art practice as more than theater or folk art, Cassel Oliver has opted to locate recent art by Black artists within a conceptual framework.

Leaving aside the question of why Piper chose this late date to register her objections,[3] is there merit to her claim that African American artists would be better served by inclusion in "multi-ethnic exhibitions"? For an artist of her stature, there is far more cachet in appearing in Documenta or Performa than in an exhibition devoted to African American art history. However, for the younger and less acknowledged artists in *Radical Presence*, a show of this kind offers an opportunity for their work to be seen in the company of artists who have successfully crossed over to the mainstream, and so to be introduced to audiences that otherwise don't seek out Black artists. By withdrawing, Piper is essentially pulling up her coattails and leaving the next generation of Black performance artists to fight the same battles for recognition anew, without the benefit of her hard-won prominence to direct attention their way.

The question remains, how is it that so many artists are still so marginalized by race, ethnicity, and even gender when many celebrity artists are women and people of color? When Louise Bourgeois and Kiki Smith are given solo exhibitions at the Guggenheim Museum and the Museum of Modern Art, respectively, why is it still necessary to have exhibitions such as the 2013 *Les Papesses* in Avignon[4] or institutions like the National Museum of Women in the Arts? To give another example, when Subodh Gupta shows with Hauser & Wirth and Anish Kapoor creates a public sculpture for London costing over thirty million US dollars,[5] why does nearly every presentation of an Indian artist in the United States appear in the context of a "contemporary art from India" exhibition? Do these groupings of artists by demographics rather than technique, subject matter, or formal concerns inadvertently limit the artists' narratives to their biographies rather than their artistic accomplishments?

Rather than answer these questions—because there is no single answer—let us instead consider why the art world continues to rely on these categories rather than simply represent a diverse spectrum of artists in the majority of exhibitions of any type. Certainly there is a marketing imperative, as shows of women, African Americans, Latinos, or artists from China and India draw audiences whose interest is in regional and social issues as well as those who support the arts. This is cause for concern only because it would seem that ethnicity- and gender-specific exhibitions have not yet had a significant effect on the exhibiting or collecting practices of mainstream art institutions in the United States. If thirty years of gains made by artists of color are not reflected in the constitution of the 2014 Whitney Biennial (in which merely 8 of the 103 artists are Black), does it stand to reason that the ethnicity exhibition is a space that is separate but not equal?

It also bears questioning whether the audience for these exhibitions comprises people who identify with the demographic or nationalist categories on view, or whether these shows are configured to introduce the typical white, upper-income art viewer to a broader scope of art. In either case, it is possible that the category in which the artist is placed is of more concern to the institution than the artwork itself. Artists from marginalized communities struggle to have their work taken on its own merits, free of essentializing rhetoric about the kind of art that people like themselves are expected to make. White, male artists, after all, are rarely if ever described as making white, male art, nor are they consigned to White Male shows (although the majority of shows remain just this). As such, exhibitions based around ethnicity reinforce the notion that whiteness is an absence of race, rather than a racial category itself. This supports the conclusion that racially marked shows are marked as such for the benefit of white audiences and institutional power players.

As Sara Ahmed says, "[O]f course whiteness is only invisible for those who inhabit it. For those who don't, it is hard not to see whiteness; it even seems everywhere. Seeing whiteness is about living its effects, as effects that allow white bodies to extend into spaces that have already taken their shape, spaces in which black bodies stand out, stand apart, unless they pass, which means passing through space by passing as white."[6] If the imperative to define ethnic histories is mandated by ongoing white supremacy in the historical and cultural mainstream, then the ethnicity exhibition operates similarly to the "Atrocity Exhibition" described by J. G. Ballard in his collection of the same name. Excluded from society and from their own artistic discourse, the asylum-bound artists whose work Ballard describes experience their prophetic visions reduced to amusements for the chattering classes. The artists remain marginalized and de-humanized to the extreme while their creative output is lauded for its raw, unconscious power. Such a condition is opposite to the intention of a curator such as Valerie Cassel Oliver, who seeks to amend the historical record to recognize the myriad contributions of Black artists to the history of performance art. Even so, Piper's response speaks to an unfortunate and ongoing reality of widespread historical marginalization on the basis of race.

1   Cembalest, "Adrian Piper Pulls Out of Black Performance–Art Show," *ArtNews*.

2   Ibid.

3   As for whether Adrian Piper would ever withdraw her work from a show that was not ethnically focused, she did withdraw her work *The Hypothesis Series* (1968–69) from Joseph Kosuth's 1970 exhibition *Conceptual Art and Conceptual Aspects* as a means of protest against the Vietnam War and the Kent State shootings. See: http://www.adrianpiper.com/art/g_hypothesis_text.shtml.

4   *Les Papesses*, which included the work of Louise Bourgeois and Kiki Smith alongside that of Camille Claudel, Jana Sterbak, and Berlinde De Bruyckere, references the story of la papesse Jeanne, who served as pope in the ninth century until it was discovered that she was pregnant. Inspired by this symbolic figure, the five female artists in the exhibition were designated the "papesses of modern and contemporary art" by the organizing museum.

5   Anish Kapoor's *ArcelorMittal Orbit* is a 376-foot sculpture and observation tower in London; it is Britain's largest piece of public art.

6   Ahmed, "Declarations of Whiteness," *Borderlands e-journal*.

Sweet and Low

Kara Walker's massive sphinx at the Domino Sugar Factory, in Brooklyn, titled *At the behest of Creative Time Kara E. Walker has confected: A Subtlety, or the Marvelous Sugar Baby, an Homage to the unpaid and overworked Artisans who have refined our Sweet tastes from the cane fields to the Kitchens of the New World on the Occasion of the demolition of the Domino Sugar Refining Plant* (2014), has been recognized mostly for Walker's hotly debated use of African American stereotypes, and for some hurtful behavior by visitors to the exhibition who Instagrammed obscene reactions to the sexually explicit central figure. Some of this is inevitable. Walker's work, marked by an oppositional aesthetics and meant to impart a strong reaction, reflects and manifests harsh realities present in the larger world. The experience of her work is raw, and some viewers experience her appropriation of racially exploitative imagery as re-traumatization irrespective of its critical intent. Such an emotional response is certainly valid. However, it is scarcely the main criteria by which the work's artistic merit should be judged.

The disrespectful behavior of some audience members is also an indication that the social codes of nudity versus nakedness of women's bodies remain more or less intact, over 150 years after Manet's *Olympia* (1863) brought them center stage. Responses to the work are further complicated by the reality of contemporary art and museum attendance (and leadership), which is overwhelmingly white, sponsorship of the installation by Domino Sugar, still linked to profit through the exploitation of Black labor, and the high-rise developer that now owns the site and whose plans are under challenge from local organizers. As such, Walker's sphinx represents an anti-slavery political statement that is itself shackled, reliant on entities that actively perpetuate the very exploitation and effacement that her narrative is intended to combat.

Walker's sphinx is in dialogue with *Olympia* much as she is with the Great Sphinx of Giza, thought to depict Pharaoh Khafre, and with the myriad (usually female) sphinxes that appear in

Symbolist painting. As she demonstrated with *After the Deluge*, her 2006 post–Katrina exhibition at the Metropolitan Museum of Art exploring the banal and catastrophic impact of water on everyday life, Walker is a student of art history. Her decision to dress the otherwise unclothed central figure in a "Mammy" head wrap relegates the sphinx to nakedness, a woman in a state of partial and thereby knowing undress who has historically been viewed as sinful, while her unselfconscious, still visually available nude counterpart has been viewed as innocent. Whiteness and Blackness are very much a part of this history, best illustrated with respect to the Odalisque tradition in art,[1] which Manet both references and modernizes.

Walker made a conscious choice to keep her sphinx wholly human in form, but her posture maintains the animalistic pose of the original sphinxes. Walker synthesizes the three figures of Manet's painting—the courtesan, her African maid, and her black cat "in heat"—amalgamating Olympia's withholding gaze, the maid's white bonnet of compliance, and the cat's crouched pose and raised tail. In her affect, Walker's sphinx is a queenly rejoinder to the wanton, man-eating sphinx of Manet's contemporaries, the Symbolists—all claws and appetite[2]—though she appears equally antagonistic to the interests of powerful men. Yet the relationship is not so simple. *A Subtlety* represents the often-contradictory interplay of desire and subjugation that drives colonization, a relationship that implicates everyone in a society in which colonial impulses are at work. Like the Sphinx of Giza, Walker's ultimately stands as a symbol of the powerful men who underwrote it—in this case, the pharaohs of capital.

The material and spatial qualities of this work far outstrip anything Walker has ever done using her characteristic medium of cut paper. Surrounding the Sphinx are *Banana Boys*, five-foot-tall cast-sugar sculptures of children who carry bundles of bananas for refining. These amber-colored, massive candies appear to serve the Sphinx like the drones of a queen bee. Over time, their translucent surfaces corrode, but their passive smiles remain. The crystallizing sugar eats away at itself, reflecting the corruption of bondage, which taints slaver and enslaved alike.

Some boys hold baskets filled with shiny, sweet fragments. Walker has explained that the "basket boys" were made in resin when the sugar casts were unsuccessful, and that they carry the remains of their shattered brethren. The candy boys are Black and Brown, their mistress recognizably Black but refined, like molasses into sugar, to a pure white. Walker has described how her interest lay in "what it means to turn sugar from brown to white and how that dovetails into becoming an American."[3]

Substitute "artist" for "American" and the work becomes a metaphor for Walker's own ascent within a contemporary art world dominated by white tastes and biases. Audiences of color who have felt themselves excluded from much of the discussion, and their interests rendered invisible by the white-centric lens of the art establishment, self-organized a recent event to highlight their differing viewpoints on *A Subtlety*. Receiving over one thousand positive RSVPs on Facebook, the event, called "We Are Here," invited people to visit the exhibition on a designated day during which organizers supplied additional context for the artwork and initiated discussion of its themes.[4]

A Subtlety is a monument to intersecting concerns of race, gender, class, and labor that inform the Domino site's history as well as the canon of art history, legacies with which many visitors were likely unfamiliar. Like any monument, *A Subtlety* is a large-scale, spectacular public artwork underwritten by the private funds of the ruling class. In this case the donors are Domino Sugar itself, representing the industry whose reliance on unpaid and underpaid labor the work critiques, and also the developers who are invested in demolishing the historic and distinctive Domino site, displacing nearby Latino families to make way for yet another faceless block of riverfront condos.

The problems posed by systems of commissioning and funding monumental art have been openly criticized by artists since the 1960s, when expanded-field artists abandoned traditional approaches to sculptural scale in favor of phenomenological, temporal, and spatial investigations. As history and taste have conferred canonical status on such dematerialized artworks, enabling the artists to realize ever more ambitious reshapings of space and time, their lack of monumentality has ceased to be reliably oppositional to capital interests—requiring ever greater investment and at times closely resembling commercial forms of property development. Walker's return to the figurative monument form in the context of a site-specific, research-centric public art project represents a completion of the circuit from monument to anti-monument. Neither figurative nor abstract monumental language can any longer be understood as implicitly antithetical to the interests of power.

For Creative Time, the non-profit public arts organization that commissioned the Walker installation, the competing interests of socially progressive contemporary art and moneyed property development are proving difficult to manage. The developer who controls the Domino site is not only a backer of the Walker project, but the co-chair of Creative Time's board, charged with helping to fund and steward the organization as a public benefit. One highly visible and positive outcome of Creative Time's strong relationships with the private sector is the emergence of Creative Time Reports, which sponsors leading artists and writers to travel and research in-depth works of reportage (though the selection of these authors in lieu of experienced journalists seems motivated more by celebrity than by investigative standards).[5] On the other hand, Creative Time has recently weathered a few controversies, including one that erupted during the run of the Walker installation when the organization came under fire from artists aligned with the BDS movement[6] for neglecting to reveal that a traveling version of their exhibition, *Living as Form* (organized for touring by Independent Curators International), had been mounted at two venues in Israel without the knowledge or consent of the participating artists, several of whom withdrew. Artists were particularly vehement about the show's second venue at the Technion, in Haifa, a university with close ties to the Israeli military and the occupation of Palestinian territories. Creative Time's official response has been that its commitment to freedom of speech prevents it from participating in what it calls "cultural boycotts," a defense that positions compliance with a US State Department agenda in Israel to serve as a progressive gloss on the ongoing civil-rights crisis in Palestine as neutrality rather than partisanship. A similar (and increasingly paltry) defense has been claimed by Kasper König, curator of the upcoming Manifesta 10 in St. Petersburg, Russia, who has come under criticism and weathered numerous artist withdrawals for continuing to maintain the viability of a socially conscious, politically progressive biennial inside an increasingly totalitarian Russian state. In both defenses, "fairness" is double-speak for complicity with repressive state interests, while accommodation of requests for support from the marginalized are characterized as "self-interest." The appetites of development, whether represented by Brooklyn condominium developers, Russian oligarchs, or the Israeli Army, trump human values despite the professed commitment to socially engaged artistic practices.

In an era when splashy blockbuster installations by well-known individual artists are consistently funded in the multi-millions while nonprofits and alternative spaces supporting countless lesser-known artists struggle to stay open, the consolidation of resources toward a single project like this one should be a reason to pause and ask questions. How does the amplification of Walker's perspective on this grand scale serve to situate her institutionalized voice as disproportionately representative of the interests of Black artists, who remain largely invisible in the contemporary art mainstream? How many working artists of color, women, and queer and transgendered artists could have had their practices substantially underwritten had the money allocated for Walker's project been distributed differently? Is Walker's work being presented with the intention of engaging new and diverse art audiences or with the goal of making homogenous and affluent art patrons appear inclusive? Whose larger agenda is such a massive investment of capital—so closely held by so few—and labor—given so cheaply by so many—truly intended to serve? The elusiveness of social parity as a priority in the arts may require the epochal ponderings of a sphinx to understand.

1   The Odalisque tradition involves the artist's depiction of a vaguely Eastern woman lying on her side as though on display for the viewer.

2   See: Allan, "Interrogating Gustave Moreau's Sphinx," *Nineteenth Century Art Worldwide*.

3   Walker, "A Sonorous Subtlety," *The Brooklyn Rail*.

4   Writing in *Colorlines*, Jamilah King describes the impetus for "We Are Here": "[T]he work has [...] provoked frustrated responses from people of color who have felt alienated by a statue so centered on the subjugation of a black woman's body. Instagram is filled with demeaning images of white people posing in front of Walker's Sphinx. That's why the 'We Are Here' event was created, said organizer Nadia Williams. 'I was really shocked about the lack of people of color [attending] this show,' said Williams, who had come to the exhibit twice before and was familiar with Walker's previous work. 'I also didn't expect all of the inappropriate visual representation that's been happening [on Instagram] and even just the lack of respect [in] how people move through the space.'" See: King, "Kara Walker's Sugar Sphinx Evokes Call From Black Women: 'We Are Here,'" *Colorlines*.

5   For Walker's exhibition, Creative Time Reports published a series of writings titled "Subtlety" that included texts by novelist Edwidge Danticat, poet Tracy K. Smith, writer and illustrator Ricardo Cortés, writer and performer Shailja Patel, and poet and novelist Jean-Euphèle Milcé.

6   BDS (Boycott, Divestment, Sanctions) describes itself as a "Palestinian-led movement for freedom, justice, and equality." See: https://bdsmovement.net/.

The Trouble with the Mission School

A panel at the San Francisco Art Institute on October 20, 2013, in conjunction with its Walter and McBean Galleries exhibition *Energy That is All Around—Mission School: Chris Johanson, Margaret Kilgallen, Alicia McCarthy, Barry McGee, Ruby Neri*, posed the question: "Mission School: Yes or No?" The general consensus, both on the panel and in the wider Bay Area arts community, was a qualified "Yes." On the panel, Natasha Boas, who curated the SFAI show, described the intense resistance with which her question—"Was there ever really a Mission School?"—was met when she began her research on an essay of the same title that was included in the UC Berkeley Art Museum's catalogue for its 2012 solo exhibition by Barry McGee. Artists refused to address the concept, objected to the label, and were otherwise evasive, even when (perhaps especially when) they had personally benefited from association with the group.

In parallel discussions within the community and on Facebook, a common response to the question was "Yes, but who cares?" Most people agree that the critical mass of artistic activity in San Francisco's Mission District in the 1990s met the social and formal criteria for a "school" of artists: shared influences and connections that congealed into apparent stylistic and material affinities and informed later generations. Why, then, does the mention of this widely recognized and influential movement in recent art history provoke a polarized response from both the artists customarily included in the group and those who are not? Understanding the hostility to the Mission School label requires an appreciation of the many ways in which this Bay Area movement prefigured controversial developments in American contemporary art and urban space over the last twenty years.

"Mission School" artists were among the first wave of young, college-educated, white and mixed-race loft dwellers to move into the historically Latino Mission District in search of cheap rent. They took inspiration and materials from the culture of the streets, incorporating found wood, graffiti, empty bottles, and hand-painted signs into paintings and installations that were by turns tragically abject and impossibly cool. The artists displayed a keen awareness even then of the problems of gentrification and cultural displacement, as evidenced by Chris Johanson's *The Survivalists* (1999). Dating from the region's first dot.com era of the late 1990s, it includes speech bubbles with snippets of conversation expressing anxiety over San Francisco housing prices and a threatened sense of community. UC Berkeley Art Museum assistant curator Dena Beard, another panelist at SFAI, described how McGee aimed to literally restore the images of people who had been priced out of the neighborhood in such works as his series of portraits done on found glass bottles. Ambivalence about the circumstances that supported their rise yet displaced their neighbors is undoubtedly one reason why these artists appear less than comfortable with their artistic association with the Mission. Compounding this is anxiety over art-world hyperbole that credits a small group with inventing ideas and styles evident in the zeitgeist that they borrowed and remixed in their works.

Boas referenced an installation at the San Francisco Museum of Modern Art in which McGee, Kilgallen, and Johanson were represented in a permanent collection display bearing an adjacent wall text that claimed the Mission School was "the most significant art movement to emerge out of San Francisco in the late twentieth century." That claim inspired her SFAI show, which seeks to expand the circle of quintessential Mission School artists to five rather than three, and to correct the gender imbalance in the SFMOMA grouping. By way of understanding the discomfort that the Mission School label provokes, imagine the embarrassment that the artists, barely in their thirties at the time of their institutional discovery, must have felt at being so sweepingly elevated into the canon of contemporary art, high above their community of teachers, mentors, and peers. The very factors that contribute to that assessment—their incorporation of a street aesthetic, their embrace of found materials and commercial techniques—are not inventions but continuations of trends that surfaced in mid-century American art by Claes Oldenburg, Robert Rauschenberg, James Rosenquist, Bridget Riley, and others, synthesized with popular art forms such as folk art and graffiti writing. Regardless of whether the Mission School represented the best of Bay Area art in the 1990s (a claim that is endlessly debatable), the group represented the aspects of Bay Area art that were most easily understood and absorbed by the New York–based art mainstream. Their departure from the rigid formalism of post-minimalist New York was a return to established concerns rather than a revolution of the sort put forward by the identity-focused and performance-oriented artists who simultaneously experienced a brief heyday.

In fact, the palatability of the Mission School's "radical" art practice for museums and galleries is the essence of its staying power. The SFAI show is unfailingly elegant and visually appealing. Despite its street pedigree, the work does not feel at all out of place in the white cube of the gallery. McCarthy, Kilgallen, and Johanson, in particular, shine in the context of an old-school painting exhibition such as this. To be sure, there can be no objection to a good-looking show, or to art that rewards viewing with pleasure. However, this represents a pre-servation of, rather than departure from, existing artistic norms. Few Bay Area or New York institutions have taken a commensurate interest in other, less marketable work from the region that has had a similarly widespread influence on younger artists. The machine performance artists Mark Pauline/Survival Research Labs, Matt Heckert, Chico MacMurtrie, Kal Spelletich, and Christian Ristow (who made the Mission their base during the 1990s); the culturally hybrid painters including Hung Liu, Enrique Chagoya, and Robert Colescott; the Mission street painters such as Rigo 23 and Eduardo Pineda; and the Latino action-based artists Carlos Villa, Guillermo Gómez-Peña, and Tony Labat have all informed the work of the Mission School artists whose renown has eclipsed theirs.

Furthermore, the ascendance of the Mission School in Bay Area art history is a fairly recent phenomenon. Critic and curator

Glen Helfand, writing in now defunct alt-weekly the *San Francisco Bay Guardian*, coined the term "Mission School" as late as 2002 to describe an art movement that was already on the wane. Jack Hanley, whose namesake gallery was on the Mission's Valencia Street from 1999 to 2009, was instrumental in bringing this work to the national stage, where it was picked up by art dealer and former museum director Jeffrey Deitch as of a piece with the new gallery-minded "street art" by artists such as Shepard Fairey and Banksy. Margaret Kilgallen's untimely death in 2001 added a layer of heartbreak to the growing myth. These are all legitimate reasons why interest in the Mission School was piqued.

The complaint from artists both within and without is less that these artists are celebrated, and more that their peers and predecessors are not. The relentless emphasis on the Mission School as the defining contemporary art movement of the Bay Area in the late twentieth century perpetuates a sense that this community does not support its own until they leave and find support elsewhere, thereby driving local talent out of town or forcing it underground. In parallel with other forms of gentrification, the success of one group whose efforts are more easily absorbed by a neoliberal economy depresses the prospects of other groups that are less readily consumed. The Mission School's elevation obscures the contributions of countless less-privileged artists whose practices are not as lucrative or deemed as valuable to an institutional system producing history in accordance with the interests of money.

Mimics and Minstrels

Two important events transpired in the art world in May of 2014 that have brought the complications of diversity and hierarchy into sharp focus. The first is the passing of Elaine Sturtevant, an artist who sublimated a critique of gendered inequity among artist peers into artworks that appropriated and re-created works deemed significant to the canon of contemporary art. The other is the withdrawal of Yams Collective, comprising thirty-eight international musicians, writers, poets, actors, and artists,[1] from the Whitney Biennial following the unsuccessful resolution of its objections to the exhibition's inclusion of a racially problematic project by artist Joe Scanlan. These two stories illustrate the challenges that appropriation-based institutional critique continues to represent for art-world institutions that are resistant to change.

Rather than address gender inequity directly in her work, Sturtevant critiqued the negotiation between economics and art history that drives the valuation of art objects. Feminism was not her stated objective; in fact, she disavowed gender's relevance to her practice. Still, it is hardly a coincidence that the artists whose works she re-created were mostly white, heterosexual men, as these were the majority of works being shown and cited among her peers. She reenacted performances and re-created objects by Marcel Duchamp, Joseph Beuys, Andy Warhol, Jasper Johns, Felix Gonzalez-Torres, and Frank Stella, among others. By her acts of remaking, she thought through the processes and experiences of the artists who made these works before her, demystifying "genius" into a collection of styles and techniques, a catalogue of contemporary practices that mirrored the distance and intellect of her own. Her work as an archivist and a re-producer prefigures important trends in contemporary art of the 1980s and 1990s by two decades.

Sturtevant was born in Ohio and came of age in New York, but the United States has been slow to embrace her. Exhibitions of her work were organized by the Serpentine Gallery, in London, the Musée Moderne de la Ville de Paris, and the Moderna

Museet, in Stockholm, over the past decade, yet the Sturtevant retrospective slated to open at the Museum of Modern Art, New York, in November 2014 will be the first museum show of her work in the United States since 1973. The wariness of American museums toward Sturtevant is surprising given their embrace of later appropriation artists, such as those of the 1980s Pictures Generation (for example, Sherri Levine and Richard Prince), but less so considering the ongoing gender disparity among artists represented in museum collections. The market continues to prefer a canon defined by individual male superstars, whom Sturtevant's whole existence reflects as negation.

Visualizing the realities of gender imbalance in the art market on a grand scale, Micol Hebron's recent *(en)Gendered (in)Equity: The Gallery Tally Poster Project* (2014), at ForYourArt in Los Angeles, included three hundred posters by different artists illustrating the gender ratios at top New York and Los Angeles galleries. The spaces Hebron and her accomplices tallied represented nearly 70 percent male artists overall. As Sturtevant's work so deftly makes clear, economic circumstance also determines whose work is deemed significant to history. As yet, no similar assessment has been made of ethnic diversity among artists represented in galleries or museums. This would seem a logical next step and one that I intend to help initiate down the line.

A 2010 report commissioned by the American Alliance of Museums indicated that the racial composition of contemporary museum audiences has remained at a level of diversity reminiscent of the 1970s while the diversity of the general population has more than tripled during that time. Worse still, comparative data shows that the percentage of people of color who are visitors to museums and art galleries has decreased as those populations have increased. For example, in 1992 the data shows that 17.5 percent of Hispanics visited museums and galleries, but in 2008 it was only 14.5 percent. Meanwhile, the population of Hispanics in the United States multiplied from 9 percent to 30.2 percent. In approximate but digestible terms, while the population of Hispanics in the United States grew from

1:10 to 1:3, the population of Hispanics among art audiences dropped from 1:5 to 1:7.[2] Similar, if less dramatic, trends are apparent among African Americans, the other group singled out in the 2008 NEA Survey of Public Participation in the Arts, cited in the AAM report.[3] Given that art-gallery and museum attendance is shown to be dropping overall, the lack of traction with growing minority populations should be a significant cause for concern within the art world. Inexplicably, the Whitney Museum has instead opted to openly alienate minority audiences in this year's Biennial.

The subject of the current controversy is Joe Scanlan's contribution to the Biennial, curated by artist and curator Michelle Grabner. Scanlan is a white man and Princeton professor whose work engages consumerism and persona in the parodic, conceptual vein mined by Sturtevant. His project for the Biennial involves creating the fictional persona of an Ivy League–educated Black female artist, "Donelle Woolford," and presenting performances and art objects conceptualized by Scanlan as the creative products of this fictional artist, played by a variety of actors. One of "Woolford's" works consists of re-performing a censored Richard Pryor stand-up routine from 1977 entitled "Dick's Last Stand," "explor[ing] the central role given to the male sexual organ in both American art and politics, perpetuating the tradition of phallic humor in popular culture."[4] Work that manipulates artistic persona is not unprecedented. Joseph Beuys and Andy Warhol self-mythologized, and many contemporary artists work under assumed or collective names, or even through simulacra. Adrian Piper's *The Mythic Being* (1973)[5] and the work of Sara Greenberger Rafferty, an artist whose critique of social roles in stand-up comedy was also selected by Grabner for inclusion in the Biennial, appear to have directly influenced Scanlan's choices. The problem with his project is that it functions by exploiting rather than critiquing the severely limited representation of minority artists at the Whitney, and in the art world more broadly. Scanlan's own name does not appear in exhibitions that include "Donelle Woolford," who is represented as if a real person. On the Whitney's artist roster, the inclusion of "Woolford" brings the number of African American participants in the Biennial to 9 out of 103 (8 percent), and the number of female participants to 38 (37 percent).[6]

The form of Scanlan's project mimics the structures by which minority voices are circumscribed and appropriated by white-dominated institutions under increasingly multicultural social conditions. Their perspectives are edited and reconstructed according to the established priorities of the dominant political class, such that their presence is ultimately represented as justification of policies that actively exclude others like them. The actors who portray "Donelle Woolford" adopt dissimilar personae, potentially critiquing the interchangeability of minority faces in an exclusionary environment. However, by maintaining that exclusionary environment, the Whitney negates any credibility it might gain from enabling the critique. Scanlan's presence as manipulator mirrors larger oppressive structures, but rather than open those structures to change, this project reinforces their inflexibility. There is simply no reason apart from institutional racism that the multiplicity of Black female perspectives that inform Scanlan's project could not be gained through an actual multiplicity of Black female artists participating in the Biennial. The fact that the Whitney prefers to present Joe Scanlan speaks volumes.

Calculated to stand out from the several dozen white male artists at the Biennial (and in every other high-profile show and job applicant pool), Scanlan uses "Woolford" to usurp the visibility accrued to minority artists in the contemporary art spotlight by the fact of their relative absence. For artists of color, that visibility is a small and hard-fought concession, a minor boost that does little to offset entrenched limitations on their access to art-world power structures. For Scanlan, the attention garnered by this project—and granted only because of the basic conditions of inequity within the exhibition and the art world—situates him to accrue benefits to his profile and market value commensurate with his position of privilege. He has parlayed this work into a professorship at Princeton (in a department where all of the tenured faculty appear to be white). He attempts to deflect the reality of that privilege by casting his fictional Black-woman persona as a person of privilege herself, as if this negates the structural power imbalance that his work exploits. (It does not.) Meanwhile, his inclusion sends a clear message to minority artists and art viewers that while the Whitney is welcoming on its face, the perspectives of people of color are subject to mediation by the white academic establishment.

Many artists and art supporters of color have already heard this message implicitly at countless exhibitions and art fairs. Yams Collective's alias HOWDOYOUSAYYAMINAFRICAN?, used for the Biennial, speaks to how pervasive the generic view of Blackness remains even in the new global art world, such that "Africa" is broadly and shallowly referenced as a historical and cultural framework, and only when compatible with a white-led agenda. Still, the inclusion of Scanlan's project at the Whitney reads as blatantly exclusionary to many people of color. Already situated as a single entity charged with representing a vast diaspora in the absence of true parity, Yams Collective ultimately chose to withdraw its work from the exhibition after failing to receive what it felt was an adequately sensitive response from the museum staff or Grabner regarding its concerns. The collective explains that its withdrawal came at the tail end of the exhibition only after it abandoned pursuing a process of dialogue and reconciliation with the institution. It was met with a response from Scanlan that underscores the tone-deaf nature of the whole undertaking. In it he justifies the "Donelle Woolford" project by extolling the educational value that producing the work has had for him personally: "I only want to say that the experiences I have had working on Donelle Woolford have been some of the most intellectually challenging and humanly rewarding experiences of my life."[7]

This self-centered perspective is at the heart of Scanlan's decision to cast Black women as agents for his personal edification and creative expression. It supersedes any concern for those women's lack of cultural space for self-determination, self-edification, or self-expression, or even whether the present undertaking further erodes that space. If Scanlan wants to make art that looks at the world from someone else's perspective, he would do better to work collectively and share the credit for his undertaking with peers who can help him broaden his own understanding rather than engage superficially through contracted performers whose influence over the project's trajectory is secondary to his own. This also requires that the Whitney value the contributions of a mixed-race group of artists as highly as it does those of a single white man. If the Biennial is to be redeemed from the obstinacy displayed by this debacle, it will only be by including a genuine diversity of artists and points of view in 2016. They could start by hiring some non-white curators next time around.

1   Leefeb, "Singular Art, Made by Plurals," *New York Times*.

2   Center for the Future of Museums, *Demographic Transformation and the Future of Museums*.

3   The full 2008 NEA Survey of Public Participation in the Arts can be found at: http://arts.gov/publications/2008-survey-public-participation-arts.

4   Whitney Museum of American Art, "Donelle Woolford: Dick's Last Stand at The Kitchen, New York | Whitney Museum of American Art."

5   The exhibition text for *Adrian Piper: The Mythic Being*, a 2016 exhibition at the Smart Museum at the University of Chicago, succinctly summarizes this project: "In 1973, Adrian Piper created an alter-ego, the Mythic Being, who became the basis of a pioneering series of performances and photo-based works. Piper—a light-skinned woman of mixed racial heritage—transformed herself into the Mythic Being by donning an Afro wig, sunglasses, and mustache and adopting behavior conventionally identified as masculine. She then explored how she and others responded to the Mythic Being. In the process, she transformed the conceptual art practices common in the period, infusing them with strong personal and political content." See: http://smartmuseum.uchicago.edu/exhibitions/adrian-piper-the-mythic-being/.

6   Steinhauer, "The Depressing Stats of the 2014 Whitney Biennial," *Hyperallergic*.

7   Heddaya, "Artist Collective Withdraws from Whitney Biennial," *Hyperallergic*.

II.

DOING WELL BY DOING GOOD

Culture, Class, and the New Economy

The 2014 election of Mayor Bill de Blasio in New York was hailed by many as a sign that the trend of economic displacement in major American urban centers was coming to an end. De Blasio ran on a progressive platform of government that serves the neediest, rather than campaign donors, and won handily on that message despite the city's prior twelve years of wealth consolidation under billionaire mayor Michael Bloomberg. Even de Blasio's art credentials[1] are more populist than those of his philanthropist predecessor, whose namesake corporation appears on the donor boards of several major institutions in the city. While many have greeted his inauguration with a level of optimism not seen since President Obama's first term, far fewer have raised the necessary question of what exactly defines the problems and the solutions we hope he will seek. Using current discussions of gentrification, shifting labor conditions, and the role of the arts in creativity and culture, I will attempt to do this here.

Artist Martha Rosler's book, *Culture Class* (2013), is a her-culean attempt to frame the scope and the terms of the gentrification debate as it concerns artists and other laborers in the new "creative economy." Her critique centers on the influential theories of Richard Florida, whose *Rise of the Creative Class* (2002) is credited with establishing that term. Rosler gained prominence in the 1970s as a conceptual photographer and video artist deconstructing the implicit social conditioning conveyed by popular images in works such as *The Bowery in Two Descriptive Systems* (1974–75) and *House Beautiful: Bringing the War Back Home* (1967–72). Her extensively researched book identifies other theorists of urban renewal, addressing their perspectives from angles of race, gender, and class. Her discussion of Florida's legacy outlines how his acolytes in business, education, and urban planning have promoted an idea of contemporary white-collar labor as a creative pursuit while promoting investment in the arts as a benefit to property values. As such, wage laborers are encouraged to consider themselves engaged in fulfilling acts of creativity rather than trading their labor for compensation. Artists are supported and valued for their ability to revitalize buildings and neighborhoods rather than for their contributions to the breadth of human experience.

This strategy has successfully reversed the long-held convention that business is politically conservative and profit oriented while art is politically liberal and concerned with the life of the mind. Instead, today one often hears that contemporary art is a space of conservatism and profiteering while industry, particularly tech, is a haven for progressive values and invention. For example, San Francisco gallerist turned entrepreneur Raman Frey suggests in a blog post that art insiders are a "community [that] views dissenters, contrarians, and critical thinkers with disdain," while technology leaders "see how value manifests from exactly these dissenters, contrarians, and critical thinkers."[2] He laments artists' perceived lack of interest in "bigger pie" thinking but never questions what the pie might be made of or that others may not want a slice. Frey is not alone in his opinions; rather, he is articulating a view shared by many in tech who cannot see why their stratospheric acquisitions of money and influence would be understood as anything but positive. Regular readers of this column will know I am no defender of art-world elitism, and some of Frey's criticisms of San Francisco's art scene ring true. However, he paints with too broad a brush, faulting artists for disdaining wealth and influence yet conflating those same artists with the old-money bloodsuckers he terms "art world bigwigs." Meanwhile, the same tech leaders that he lauds for recognizing the value of dissent have yet to acknowledge the validity of criticisms leveled by many within the communities their employees are rapidly displacing.

A crucial distinction here is the one between artist and designer, which Rosler makes but Frey does not. This is best expressed by art critic Ben Davis in his book *9.5 Theses on Art and Class*. Davis writes, "The opposition between art and design here is above all a difference between two different class-based notions of creative labor."[3] Davis suggests that we ought to define "working class" and "middle class" based not on earnings, but on relative autonomy of the worker. By his equation, a low-paid artist might be a member of the "middle class" because she sets her own schedule, decides which projects to complete and in what order of priority, and creates products (works of art) according to her own interests and specifications, only introducing them to a market when they are complete. A highly paid engineer might be a member of the "working class" because she works assigned hours, chooses and prioritizes projects based on management imperatives, puts her labor for hire on the open market, and creates products according to the needs and conditions of clients or end users. This configuration shocks many artists who have aligned themselves politically with the working class and the poor, as it surely does many engineers endowed with cars, homes, and disposable income. However, while CEOs of technology companies and their youngest employees may wholly believe in their own autonomy and their radical break from the past, many tech workers in their thirties and forties have come up against company hierarchies and policies designed to let them know when their quest for self-determination runs counter to the will of their superiors. The lucky few have enough money put aside to quit and pursue their own agendas, including art. The majority are just barely hanging on in cities where a low six-figure salary is barely sufficient to meet middle-class expectations of home ownership and parenthood.

Historian and political analyst Michael Parenti writes that "[y]ou will have no sensation of a leash around your neck if you sit by the peg. It is only when you stray that you feel the restraining tug."[4] Perhaps the most resonant criticism of gentrification's effects on urban communities is that the increased wealth of new arrivals is matched by increasing ethnic and social homogeneity. The new creative economy disproportionately benefits the same people who benefited from the old order: white, college-educated males from families already privy to some degree of economic and social influence. Given that the interests of this group are already aligned with the interests of the ruling class, it is no wonder that so many of them believe themselves unleashed. Their entire orbits circulate around the peg. This reality renders claims of "disruption" hollow, in that one cannot truly disrupt that on which one wholly depends. In this context, the only ethnic and gender minorities who can excel are those whose class status situates them near the peg as well, and the only critiques that gain traction are ones that position this privileged class as a solution to rather than a source of social problems.

Rebecca Solnit has written at length about the tangible effects of the creative economy on San Francisco, symbolized by the newly ubiquitous "Google Bus." Writing in the *London Review of Books*, she describes the vehicles: "Most of them are gleaming white, with dark-tinted windows, like limousines, and some days I think of them as the spaceships on which our alien overlords have landed to rule over us."[5] She links the imperialist underpinnings of contemporary tech with respect to privacy and data security to tech companies' fraught relationships with the communities that surround them. She is undoubtedly correct to raise the alarm regarding Google's, Facebook's, and others' relentless quest to monetize our attention and market our personal data. She is also on point with her assessment that the new, young creative professionals moving in are technologically wired but socially disconnected. She makes a few missteps as well, for example ascribing certain antisocial behaviors to technology workers as a class that could be explained equally by the relative youth and immaturity of the new arrivals. For someone with as long a history in San Francisco and the Bay Area as Solnit, it is surprising to hear her talk about the current rent boom as a wholly new phenomenon when it is clearly the second round of a cycle that began in the 1990s. Even so, Solnit has used her high profile to bring attention to the negative effects of San Francisco's Richard Florida–esque transformation. Even more than New York, San Francisco is a city identified with the creative economy, and one where the very counterculture that gentrification has displaced is continually dangled in front of new recruits as evidence of their own ingenuity and autonomy within the corporate system.

The mythology of the creative economy explains much of why San Franciscans who have pioneered this approach to work are under-invested in the arts despite some apparent affinities. Why support artists with your hard-earned income when you are fully convinced you are an artist yourself, and a more valuable one? Why make the effort to understand artists' concerns as grounded in history and social justice, when it is more comfortable to characterize them, as Frey puts it, as encumbered by "suspicion of wealth, fame, and influence"?[6] Solnit takes the opposite position: "The problem is that we understand Silicon Valley's values all too well, and a lot of us don't like them."[7] While history has produced scores of artists who also sit close to the peg, the avant-garde tradition includes a healthy measure of informed political and social dissent. Technology and design entrepreneurs have engaged in politics to further industry interests such as net neutrality and looser immigration policies, but have done little to create a space for public dialogue and social critique that would rival the efforts put forth by artists in this regard.

1   Grynbaum, "De Blasio Brings Hope for a Populist Arts Revival," *New York Times.*

2   Frey, "Art and Tech in the Bay Area," *Medium.*

3   Davis, "Art and Class," *9.5 Theses on Art and Class.*

4   Parenti, *Dirty Truths.*

5   Solnit, *London Review of Books.*

6   Frey, "Art and Tech."

7   Solnit, "Welcome to the (Don't Be) Evil Empire: Google Eats the World," *TomDispatch.*

#PLACE   #LABOR   #CLASS   #GENTRIFICATION   #TECHNOLOGY   #ACCESS

The Business End of Art

As in nearly every field of commerce, it seems that the tension between old and new models of the business of art is coming to a head. Traditional galleries see that their established methods of selling selectively and covertly to buyers of high social standing are under threat. Museums, once beneficiaries of philanthropic largesse from those same well-heeled collectors, now often find that their leading patrons are competitors: rather than donate their holdings, they establish private institutions instead—like LA's Broad Museum, opening September 2015—that rival the scale and scope of the Moderns and Contemporaries, which are left empty-handed. Even major gifts to museums, such as the unrivaled Fisher Collection, now entrusted to the San Francisco Museum of Modern Art, come with strict and costly requirements, such as new buildings and capital campaigns. Meanwhile, the most visible and valuable contemporary artists are no longer those who have been vetted by scholars and curators, but those whose works can be most readily flipped on the secondary and auction markets. Under these circumstances, the art object is purely a marker of exchange value upon which certain complicit thinkers heap vague claims of cultural use value that seem to apply only to the acquisitive culture of the 1%.

The anxiety of the old guard toward the new manifests most clearly in the recent *New York Times* and *Observer* profiles of art impresario Stefan Simchowitz (tellingly titled "The Art World's Patron Satan" and "Stefan Simchowitz vs. the Art World," respectively). Simchowitz has a venture-capital and film production background, a Los Angeles aesthetic, and a start-up approach to artists, dumping money into new and unproven talent so as to play the odds that some of the artists he supports will reach the upper echelons of the market and bear out his investments as a group. Both profiles describe a man who sees himself as an underdog and, as belies his tech-funding background, a "disrupter" of established systems.[1] His critics, who include several prominent dealers, call him a "flipper" who takes advantage of emerging artists while devaluing their output for personal profit. His champions see him as a person willing to take a risk on an unproven artist in an era when few collectors seem to value that kind of patronage.

Simchowitz's methods can be troubling. His relationship to emerging artists is more paternalistic than paternal, and his tendency to hoard artists' works and then liquidate them in large numbers when an artist's market peaks (known as "flooding the market") is potentially damaging to a young artist's longevity. Still, his claim in the *Observer* that the art world "weaponized me"[2] rings true. After all, Simchowitz did not create an art-school system that neglects to teach young artists how to manage their financial and personal affairs, or a gallery system that treats artists as freelance content creators without health care or a steady source of income. He is simply exploiting structures that were engineered to engender exploitation. Jerry Saltz, writing with typically dated bluster on *Vulture*, calls Simchowitz a "Sith Lord." Simchowitz's language, he claims, is that "of people who pass through the art world on their way from one industry to another. They bring their skill set, honed on IPOs and flips, to make some fast money, draw attention, and gain social currency."[3] The implication that Saltz (whom the public may remember from that paragon of integrity, the reality TV show *Work of Art*) is a Jedi knight by comparison, conveniently obscures the critic's track record of championing artists of what Hito Steyerl calls "shiny instability," "baffled and mesmerized" by "the not-so-discreet consumer-friendly veneer of new and old oligarchies, and plutotechnocracies."[4] In other words, the debate is less black hat/white hat, and more shades of gray.

Meanwhile, the onslaught of the "creative economy" continues unabated. Lumping artists in with designers, entertainers, and producers, this line of thinking focuses exclusively on the economic power of creative work while eliding questions of culture, ethics, and precarious or contingent labor. Artists are valued because they create economic value, not because the work they do is valuable. Government and foundation grants are increasingly bound up in this rhetoric and the related discourse of "creative placemaking," which essentially codifies artists' heretofore inadvertent role in the march of urban gentrification.[5] Meanwhile, artists are rarely the beneficiaries of the economic growth they are credited with generating. According to the 2014 Otis Report on the Creative Economy, "In the visual and performing arts, there were nearly 2.7 self-employed persons in Los Angeles County for every salaried worker."[6] In 2012, the report shows that 64,108 self-employed visual artists and writers earned a cumulative total of $2,645,500,000, or an average of $41,266 per capita in annual earnings in a county where the median household income was $55,909 according to the US Census. This means that more than two-thirds of the self-employed artists and writers in Los Angeles County, representing almost 1.75 workers to every 1 salaried worker in the visual and performing arts, are earning lower-than-average wages. "Creativity" is being celebrated as a profit center, but artists are still being starved.

What, then, is the alternative for artists who want to control their own careers and finances? One option is to embrace the label of "entrepreneur," which some have done, such as stARTup Art Fair organizers Steve Zavattero (formerly of San Francisco gallery Marx & Zavattero) and Ray Beldner (an artist and promoter),[7] though not without criticism. Writing for SFMOMA's *Open Space*, Bean Gilsdorf and Joseph del Pesco critiqued the "independent" San Francisco hotel fair, not only for its pay-to-play model that charges artists exhibitor fees based on the cost of gallery fairs, but for lacking "a sense of dignity," calling self-identification by artists as "'entrepreneurs' or 'creative visionaries'" "hollow self-nominations" and "clichés of corporate culture."[8] Certainly, the promise of entrepreneurship puts a positive gloss on numbers like the ones cited above, framing precarious employment as a choice rather than a condition of, as the Otis report puts it, "competitive pressures stemming from globalization" that "continue to exert enormous pressure on firms to cut costs," leading to "companies seeking efficiencies by using more part-time and temporary labor, and outsourcing non-core tasks to independent contractors."[9]

Convincing artists that they are entrepreneurs can be a way of flattering them while exploiting them, as Gilsdorf and del Pesco suggest.

At the same time, critics like Ben Davis have pointed out that artists have long operated in the economic space of entrepreneurs: self-employed, running sole proprietorships or small workshops, retaining intellectual-property rights, seeking angel investors, and ultimately rejecting a corporate mentality that values true entrepreneurship only when it can acquire and consume independent actors, subjugating them to hierarchies of rank and social privilege that are hardly alien to the institutional art world. What, then, of the artist who aspires to loftier goals than mere economic success? This is a particularly thorny challenge given that art objects and, increasingly, performative and intervention-based events are readily commoditized in our culture. In his 2012 Avenali Lecture for the Townsend Center for the Humanities at UC Berkeley, literary theorist Frederic Jameson spoke of how the art object is no longer the focal point of creative production, but rather functions in the marketplace as a derivative of an event-based spectacle much like pork futures operate as derivatives of factory pig-farming. This perspective goes a long way toward explaining why both a corporate raider like Simchowitz would turn from tech funding to contemporary art speculation and an artist like Oscar Murillo, whom Simchowitz claims to have discovered, would downplay the popularity of his market-friendly abstract paintings of late and turn to creating spectacles of labor, such as the facsimile of a Colombian chocolate factory that he staged, complete with imported workers, at David Zwirner, in New York, in 2014. Installations of this kind allow an artist like Murillo, raised in the working class, to engage with issues of class and race that resurface in the context of artistic labor, while creating a pretense of social responsibility that a savvy gallerist can use as large-scale promotion for the artist's lucrative paintings. At the same time, one can see the twenty-eight-year-old Murillo struggling to bolster himself against the capricious market, which he knows will toss him aside as quickly as it lauded him, by branching out into more academically respectable spaces of artistic production than the trendy abstractions that have branded him "a new Basquiat."[10]

A safe haven for artists would relieve them of such anxieties by providing adequate economic support for creative labor to liberate it from market whims, but that is not currently a possibility in these United States. Without a guarantee of healthcare, basic sustenance, and social investment in artists and art institutions—as one finds in Germany or Canada—artists are left to negotiate a winner-take-all system of profit and speculation to the best of their ability. In this country, the art economy mirrors the whole of the economy, while the academic art establishment remains heavily invested in denying the relevance of business concerns to artists' education while prioritizing those concerns in every other aspect of their operations. Questions of the business of being an artist, from managing personal finances to finding a gallery that will actually work for their 50 percent cut, to juggling part-time employment and a daily studio practice, are neglected in favor of idealism in most art departments despite the unsustainable number of newly minted MFA graduates and the exorbitant cost of an art education.[11] Instead, debt becomes another way that young artists are disciplined into toeing the neoliberal line and abandoning the radical politics of many of their predecessors. I can't see how artists could be further harmed by seizing control of the business apparatus that is clearly going to affect them whether or not they take an active role in their own financial affairs. If the future of art patronage resembles Stefan Simchowitz's approach, the most successful artist will be the one who knows how to make capital work for her, rather than working for capital.

1   Christopher Glazek writes in the *New York Times*: "To his detractors, Simchowitz is the Michael Milken of the art world—someone who has created, through his extensive network and force of personality, a market for high-risk, high-yield investments that have little to do with the fundamentals of talent and critical acclaim. By contrast, Simchowitz sees himself as something akin to the art world's Mark Zuckerberg, a 21st-century player using technology to disrupt the institutional establishment." See: Glazek, "The Art World's Patron Satan," *New York Times Magazine*.

2   Duray, "Stefan Simchowitz vs. the Art World," *Observer*.

3   Saltz, "Saltz on Stefan Simchowitz, the Greatest Art-Flipper of Them All," *Vulture*.

4   Steyerl and Jordan, "Hito Steyerl, Politics of Post-Representation," *dis magazine*.

5   "In creative placemaking, partners from public, private, non-profit, and community sectors strategically shape the physical and social character of a neighborhood, town, city, or region around arts and cultural activities [...] animat[ing] public and private spaces, rejuvenat[ing] structures and streetscapes, improv[ing] local business viability and public safety, and bring[ing] diverse people together to celebrate, inspire, and be inspired. In turn, these creative locales foster entrepreneurs and cultural industries that generate jobs and income [...]" See: Markusen and Gadwa, *Creative Placemaking*.

6   Los Angeles County Economic Development Corporation, 2014 *Otis Report on the Creative Economy*.

7   Begun in San Francisco in 2015, the stARTup Art Fair has become, as of 2017, an annual event in San Francisco, Chicago, and Los Angeles. See: https://www.startupartfair.com/.

8   Del Pesco and Gilsdorf, "What's up with stARTup?," *Open Space*.

9   Los Angeles County Economic Development Corporation, 2014 *Otis Report on the Creative Economy*, 26.

10 Swanson, "How Oscar Murillo Perfectly Encapsulates the Current State of the Contemporary Art World," *Vulture*.

11 For more on the realities and prospects of graduates in the arts, explore the work of BFAMFAPHD, a collective of artists, designers, technologists, organizers, and educators invested in cultural equity and interested in the effects of student loan debt and financial precarity on the "lives of creative people." It creates reports and pedagogical tools that it publishes on http://bfamfaphd.com/.

Education on Contingency

This past May Day week (2014), there has been much chatter about the decision by adjunct faculty at the San Francisco Art Institute (SFAI) to file for a union election. This comes on the heels of a similar decision to file for union election by Mills College adjuncts and the formation of a union to represent adjuncts at the Maryland Institute College of Art. The ubiquity of adjuncts in college teaching is not new, but the conversation around unions for part-time faculty has emerged more recently. Meanwhile, tensions regarding low pay and lack of job security and benefits for instructors, and rising tuition costs for students, are finally converging to invigorate a public conversation about the substandard working conditions of the majority of American college faculty.[1]

In the arts, this overreliance on a precarious labor force is doubly appalling, given that much contemporary art rhetoric draws heavily on a Marxist construction of labor that resists and opposes alienation of workers in the interests of capital. For such intellectual constructs to be transmitted to new generations of artists and students by a fundamentally alienated workforce of adjuncts is a genuine scandal. The renewed emphasis on collectivity in art that coincides with the emergence of social and pedagogical post-conceptual practices seems not to be reflected in the values of academic institutions such as SFAI. This is evident in president Charles Desmarais's appeal to adjunct faculty to reject the Service Employees International Union's efforts to unionize them, which was criticized by longtime visiting faculty (aka adjunct) Dale Carrico in a cogent blog post that called out the school for touting its Diego Rivera mural while discouraging contingent employees from organizing.[2] Rivera's famously working-class politics may seem a historical footnote to administrators, but for faculty and students, they are again relevant. Consider, after all, that the newly minted MFAs graduating from these non-unionized, adjunct-heavy art schools will face the same enormous pressure to comply with an unfair system that the adjuncts who teach them currently contend with.

#LABOR #AFFECTIVE #PRECARITY #MFA #UNIONS #ADJUNCTS

As schools struggle to accommodate an increasingly global student body, the faculty who most represent and can mentor those students are consistently among those whose situations are most precarious. In the *New Yorker* blog, novelist Junot Díaz describes how alienated he felt in his own MFA program in the early 1990s because no faculty resembled him or knew of canonical texts by artists of color. He writes, "I was a person of color in a workshop whose theory of reality did not include my most fundamental experiences as a person of color—that did not in other words include me."[3] To the extent that American academic institutions have corrected for this absence since then, it has largely been through hiring adjunct faculty from under-represented groups to balance the perspectives of older, white, tenured faculty. Rather than inspire a student like Díaz to excel, their circumstances demonstrate that while people of color may have a presence, the academy is not committed to their success.

Artist and writer Christian Nagler, visiting faculty in SFAI's Interdisciplinary Studies and New Genres departments, led a workshop at the UC Berkeley Arts Research Center's April 2014 practicum *Valuing Labor in the Arts* titled "Yoga for Adjuncts." Alternating between facilitating a conventional yoga class and lecturing on labor, policy, and philosophy as related to economic precarity, Nagler led a group of educators, curators, and artists through our paces while asking us to question our assumptions about work and reward. As we wrapped, lingering in the refreshing pause of corpse pose, I was struck by the rarity of such a moment of peace in the lived experience of the adjunct. Dashing from one school to the next over sometimes substantial distances, veteran educators and dedicated artists exhaust themselves daily to cobble together a subsistence living while somehow, inexplicably, drawing the energy to inspire and enlighten students. The pace can be untenable, and some, like myself, choose to abandon teaching for full-time opportunities elsewhere. That choice to leave students and institutions of higher learning represents a profound loss, even if the alternative supplies much-needed financial stability.

Adjuncting as a supplement to work in the field remains acceptable, but adjuncting as a way of life has become a trap for too many talented teachers and thinkers. Perhaps the recent efforts to unionize will go some way toward improving what is presently a dismal situation.

1   An April 2014 report by the American Association of University Professors showed that "adjuncts now constitute 76.4 percent of US faculty across all institutional types, from liberal-arts colleges to research universities to community colleges. A study released by the US House of Representatives in January reveals that the majority of these adjuncts live below the poverty line," reports Elizabeth Segran, in the *Atlantic*. See: Segran, "The Adjunct Revolt: How Poor Professors Are Fighting Back," *Atlantic*.

2   Dale Carrico's post concludes with the provocative call for SFAI administrators to "sandblast Diego Rivera's fresco from the gallery wall for they are already blind to its beauty and its wisdom." See: Carrico, "San Francisco Art Institute Touts Diego Rivera Fresco Celebrating Labor Politics While Engaging in Union Busting," *Amor Mundi*.

3   Díaz, "MFA vs. POC," *New Yorker*.

Punk Is Dead, Long Live Punk

Is the *Metropolitan Museum of Art's Punk: Chaos to Couture* (2013) the death knell of punk as a social and cultural movement? Certainly, the Met's assertion that the locus of punk's importance is in its influence on high fashion would indicate that it is no longer relevant to these larger concerns. The A-list attendees at May's opening gala were decidedly mainstream and largely advocates for materialistic values. Sarah Jessica Parker, whose iconic *Sex and the City* character relentlessly equated emancipation with consumption, was the event's poster child. She drew attention from both art and celebrity gossip media with a fauxhawk designed by Philip Treacy, a milliner whose rise to fame has depended on the support of the same royal family that the Sex Pistols skewered with "God Save the Queen" back in 1977.

The exhibition makes the pretense of celebrating punk as a historical moment, but it fails to establish historical context. Like the replicas of CBGB's men's room and Vivienne Westwood and Malcolm McLaren's Chelsea boutique, history itself has been sanitized and aired out. Little mention is made of the crushing poverty and urban blight that nearly destroyed both New York and London in the 1970s, prompting young people with few prospects to take up a nihilistic, antagonistic posture symbolized by a violent, abject aesthetic. No mention at all is made of Black cultural influence, from Rude Boys to Sharps, on the punk style and ethic.

The parallels with our own era are all too clear. Then, as now, economic and social elites flaunted their wealth while average people struggled to gain education and employment in the shadow of prolonged and expensive overseas wars. People lost faith in government and institutions, revolutions roiled the Global South, and gas prices soared. People of color found their cultural contributions absorbed and erased by the white mainstream. Yet while Queen Elizabeth II's Silver Jubilee in 1977 sparked parody and revolt, last year's Diamond Jubilee protests were fairly tame and skewed much older. Punk in the 1970s provided an artistic and social outlet for the youth whom society was failing. Today it would seem to be just another fad, notable for its influential style and innovative materialism but stripped of its conscience.

What is punk's appeal to couturiers? The Met argues that punk's use of post-industrial materials and unconventional symmetries inspires fashion designers. However, these elements have their own provenance in Process Art, Dada, Gutai, and Neo-Concretism, all of which are canonical art movements that predate the 1970s. There is a deeper reason why punk has been selected to get the Met's revisionist treatment, aside from its global appeal as a major movement in rock music and graphic art. Punk's anti-corporate message and its anarchic ethic have as much pull on the public imagination as ever, and the only bulwark against their power is that public's collective amnesia. The Met has seized on a perfect narrative, one that defangs punk's political relevance and frames its influence as limited to specific (Western) geographies and (bygone) eras. By doing so, the museum and the fashion houses it represents here can appeal to the 1% and its appetite for cultural appropriation and regurgitation while rendering an oppositional movement impotent and excising its practitioners from the narrative. It's no accident that Debbie Harry is the only living punk artist in gala photographs, which feature manufactured celebrities like Katy Perry and Miley Cyrus doing clichéd Sid Vicious impersonations.

Punk was a DIY movement that sprung up in opposition to the hippies but held many similar values. Among these were communal living in self-organizing "punk house" communes and a post-Marxist quest for connection to the fruits of one's labor through craft. Making is a critical aspect of the punk ethos, which celebrates individuality and resourcefulness in expressing it. The display of early T-shirts by Westwood demonstrates how closely punk was connected to a working-class history of agitprop printmaking. The Met show features dresses made from plastic bags (Maison Martin Margiela, Moschino) or sprayed with paint (Alexander McQueen,

Anne Demeulemeester) and adorned with hundreds of safety pins and studs. The look and feel of the clothes is often spot-on, but the sense of acquisitive desire that they invoke in the viewer is antithetical to punk's call to create rather than consume.

Most importantly, by locating punk's significance solely at its origin as a European-American movement of the 1970s, the Met exhibition overlooks punk's continued value as an egalitarian ethos of the young, opposed to the greed and totalitarianism of the old. Nowhere is punk more relevant today than in the Islamic world. Teens in Indonesia have been subjected to forced head-shaving and re-education for wearing punk fashion in recent years. Inspired by the Riot Grrrl stylings of Ukrainian protest group FEMEN, Tunisian feminist activist Amina Sboui created a furor earlier this year for posting images of herself online, topless and sporting a bleached-blond punk haircut à la Wendy O. Williams, the Plasmatics singer known for on-stage theatrics such as partial nudity and occasional explosions. *Beats for Bangladesh*, a compilation featuring US-based Taqwacore and South Asian hip-hop acts, was recently released to benefit survivors of the 2013 Rana Plaza fire in Bangladesh, which brought dismal overseas working conditions in the fashion industry to international attention. These cases make clear that punk is more than a Western cultural export for consumption; it is a wake-up call to youth that they must take their futures into their own hands. Mass protests in Egypt and Turkey are part of the same awakening, prompted by anger at corrupt govern-ments and reactionary beliefs. In the Global South, revolution remains imperative. We may have forgotten why punk was invented, but it's reinvented every day.

Divide//Conquer: Artists Confront the Gentrification of Urban Space

Any conversation among artists these days is bound to turn to the question of gentrification—the process of urban renewal by private developers that ultimately displaces poor residents in favor of the upwardly mobile. Modernism in art has always accompanied displacement of poor citizens from city centers, from the time of the Impressionists, when Georges-Eugène Haussmann refashioned Paris's boulevards, parks, and public works, to the remaking of Manhattan as a banker's playground under committed arts philanthropist Michael Bloomberg. As the present-day wealth gap spreads and assets are increasingly concentrated in the hands of the wealthiest Americans, artists and activists find themselves on the front lines of a nation-wide battle to preserve the characteristics of ethnic and bohemian neighborhoods from the homogenizing forces of corporate culture.

Activists engaged in political struggles defined along economic, racial, and sociological lines have an established part to play in defending against this onslaught, and a clear justi-fication for their involvement in protest actions and legal challenges. Artists, on the other hand, have a more ambivalent relationship to these trends. They are often implicated as both the perpetrators and the victims of gentrification. Many believe that their role is not to speak out about social issues but to communicate self-expression. They are experts in neither legal nor civic arenas. Given these truths, how and why should artists engage in the fight to save urban communities from eviction and displacement?

To understand why artists are compelled to participate in these struggles, first consider how gentrification occurs. An area subject to prolonged neglect is often the only affordable location for recent immigrants, the working poor, and other marginalized groups to reside. Their presence fosters further civic neglect, as these are groups with minimal political clout that remain invisible to many politicians and business leaders.

Many artists of note have emerged from within these ostracized communities, informed by their vernacular traditions and inspired to create positive images and messages to counter the symptoms of neglect. In recent history, these have included founders of graffiti art, mural art, performance art, and interventionist art movements that have transformed mainstream art discourse. Other artists move into these areas because they too have limited means, and find not only cheap rents but a sense of safety in community to guard against the hardships of urban poverty. Eventually, the energizing force of artistic creation helps to revive these atrophied regions despite the lack of civic or capital investment, at which point developers take notice and begin to snatch up the remaining inexpensive or abandoned properties. Those newly renovated properties are marketed to the professional class with the vibrant local culture as a major selling point. As upscale residents move in, the creators whose works helped create interest in these areas often find themselves priced out along with their less affluent neighbors.

Despite their involvement in all aspects of this process, artists are generally on the side of the displaced in the gentrification debate. This has been the case in San Francisco, where the long-standing creative denizens of the Mission District are particularly vocal opponents of urban development in its current form. Recently the impending eviction of artists René Yañez and Yolanda Lopez has made headlines, prompting artists around the Bay Area to rally for these two doyens of the Chicano Movement.[1] In an open letter to Yañez distributed via social media networks, internationally recognized performance artist Guillermo Gómez-Peña used his considerable influence to draw broader attention to the plight of Latino residents in the Mission and around San Francisco who have of late been subjected to unprecedented numbers of Ellis Act evictions.[2] Outrage is high among the city's established and visible creators, as articulated by iconic Bay Area author Rebecca Solnit, who writes, "Adding newcomers might not be so bad if it didn't mean subtracting a lot of those of us who are already here. By us I mean everyone who doesn't work for a gigantic technology corporation or one of the smaller companies hoping to become a global monolith [...] People at various income levels in a diversity of fields here in San Francisco are being replaced by those who work in one field and get paid extremely well. Small, alternative, and nonprofit institutions are also struggling and going down."[3] Nonetheless, the rhetoric coming from developers is that the incoming affluent types are in fact themselves "creative" workers who will contribute to, rather than detract from, the vitality of these remade neighborhoods. The redefinition of "creativity" along corporate lines contributes to the vast cultural divide between the Bay Area's haves and have-nots.

As the booming tech industry displaces scores of longtime residents, it is tempting to direct ire at the corporations who attract and generate all of this new money. Filipina performance art collective Mail Order Brides/M.O.B. (artists Jenifer Wofford, Eliza Barrios, and Reanne Estrada) have satirized the winner-take-all mentality of Silicon Valley with *Manananggoogle* (2013–ongoing), a work commissioned by the San Jose Museum of Art in which the three portray high-powered female executives in the mode of *Lean In* author and Facebook COO Sheryl Sandberg, and Marissa Mayer, formerly a Google executive and the CEO of Yahoo! Jenifer "Baby" Wofford, Eliza "Neneng" Barrios, and Reanne "Immaculata" Estrada performed *Divide// Conquer: The Manananggoogle Onboarding Experience* as part of *The Long Conversation* (2013), an exhibition commemorating long-standing alternative art space Southern Exposure's impending thirty-ninth anniversary. This occasion is made more monumental by the truth of how few spaces founded in that germinating moment of the 1970s are still around and fiscally sustainable. Incorporating found video, text, live performance, and social intervention, M.O.B. applies a mode of cannibalistic appropriation derived from Latin American Modernist precedents to a contemporary milieu in which the primitive and the futuristic are both intertwined and interchangeable.

M.O.B.'s characters are funhouse distortions who give the lie to common multinational rhetoric in which all of the world's problems are anticipated to be solved by the Westernization

#NEOCOLONIALISM　#INDUSTRY　#TECHNOLOGY　#CLASS　#RACE　#DISPLACEMENT　#GENTRIFICATION

and capitalization of women and people of color. The slogan, "Divide Conquer," applies equally to the neo-colonial aspirations of American tech multinationals as to the *manananggal* herself, a Filipino folk demon that splits her top half from her human bottom to manifest as a Harpy-like vampire. Wofford, Barrios, and Estrada comically marry the mythos of the manananggal with the team-building management rhetoric of corporate America to demonstrate that it is the system and not the participants that bears the blame for widespread rapacity. That point was driven home at the event hosted by the Global Fund for Women, in which audience members were divided by gender. Women were humorously encouraged to take up space and express power while men were mock-trained to be servile and obsequious in a reversal of the traditional gender hierarchy. Despite everyone being in on the joke, it was notable how the tone of the crowd shifted from one of community-art collegiality toward raw competition with just a little encouragement. The result fell somewhere between the Dunder Mifflin Office Olympics and a low-stakes Stanford Prison Experiment. The parody was maintained through hilarious commentary from Wofford (the Bay Area's Pinay Lucille Ball), Estrada (playing a CEO-cum-dominatrix), and Barrios (in a fright wig nearly as scary as the manananggal). Jokes aside, the point was well made that neo-colonialism is as much in evidence in the transformation of our own communities as in the actions of multinationals abroad.

Despite such clear objections from artists to the ongoing development of our cities at any cost, it is by no means certain that contemporary art as a culture industry is opposed to gentrification. Property development is the order of the day for any museum wishing to establish itself as worthy of national and international attention. Many boards of art institutions are manned by developers and captains of industry, while affluent and homogenous urban populations are more likely to share the nineteenth-century world views of many high-profile curators. Meanwhile, the alternative and community-driven spaces that indigenous and immigrant communities and socially marginalized groups have historically created to support themselves, financially and as proponents of free expression, are shuttering at an alarming rate. Gentrification affects not only individuals and families, but cultural institutions as well. Particularly vulnerable are those that came about in the 1970s and 1980s, thanks to NEA funding that is no longer available, to serve populations that have since been dispersed. The great tragedy of gentrification, which its proponents appear not to recognize, is that groups that are displaced can never be reunited in another, more affordable location. Instead, the critical mass that drove cultural innovation and fostered community is lost permanently, and with it, the collective energy that drives our most essential artistic developments.

1   René Yañez is credited with "seed[ing] and gr[owing] the annual Dia de Los Muertos celebration into a citywide event," and is the founder of iconic Mission organizations the Mission Cultural Center and Galería de la Raza. Yolanda Lopez, a painter, printmaker, and educator, was part of the 1968 strike at San Francisco State University and is best known for her Virgin de Guadalupe series of drawings, paintings, collage, and prints. See: Mack, "Royalty of the Mission Art Scene Faces Eviction," *Mission Local.*

2   In the period between March 1, 2015, and February 29, 2016, Ellis Act evictions, in which a building owner evicts tenants with the intention of taking the building off the market, accounted for 154 of the 2,134 total evictions in San Francisco. up 36 percent from the previous years' Ellis Act evictions. See: Morse, "Report: Ellis Act Filings Up 36% As Evictions Hit Six-Year High," *SFist.*

3   Solnit, "Welcome to the (Don't Be) Evil Empire: Google Eats the World," *TomDispatch.*

#NEOCOLONIALISM   #INDUSTRY   #TECHNOLOGY   #CLASS   #RACE   #DISPLACEMENT   #GENTRIFICATION

III.

THE IMMANENT PUBLIC

The Painting

So much hinges on the question of audience. Who is presumed to engage with artwork, and on what terms? In the museum, people of color so often feel that we are not the intended audience. The hurt that we experience on realizing that disconnect—that we are here for art but art is not necessarily here for us—has now been made starkly evident by a clumsy gesture that instigated so much debate that it seems to overpower any other conversation. This is a feeling we expect to get at the 2017 Whitney Biennial on a regular basis, and it is why so many people were negatively affected simply by the image of the painting as it circulated around the internet. It's all the more frustrating when one stands before the painting, feeling the weakness of its impact and the pull of the other artists' works around it.

Perhaps what surprises most about seeing the painting in person is how small it is. Henry Taylor's *Ancestors of Genghis Khan with Black Man on Horse* (2015–17), on the sixth-floor landing, is many times its size. Nearly obscured in a back corner of a fifth-floor gallery, the now-infamous painting of Emmett Till does not scream for attention the way Dana Schutz's other paintings on the fifth floor do. If anything, it is not sensational enough—not visceral enough, not cruel enough to do justice to its subject. On a large and busy floor, featuring a dizzying vortex by Samara Golden, Pope.L's oozing bologna slices, a 3-D film by Anicka Yi, and works using the institution to illustrate the operations of capital from Occupy Museums and Cameron Rowland, the painting seems an ancillary work in the curatorial argument. This is perhaps the biggest indictment, this and its utter lack of resolution. Above these galleries hang several luxurious handmade banners by Cauleen Smith. "Rage blooms within me," they proclaim. "I am holding my breath." "We were never meant to survive." Maya Stovall's four videos of public performances in the streets of Detroit hang adjacent to the painting. In them, people of color talk about their experiences and their dreams. It is possible to hear their voices while looking directly at the painting of Emmett Till.

Looking at the painting is difficult. The obvious challenge is the subject matter, and how it clashes unnervingly with the candy-like color scheme. Neo-Expressionism's blend of grotesque and provocative subject matter, combined with the media-saturated palette of Pop Art, makes a style particularly ill-suited for rendering an image of raw horror. Certainly the effect seems facile—if not exactly glib, then more ambivalent and anxious than the subject warrants. Critics of the painting have charged that it violates an innate truth carried in the original photograph. What is that truth, and is it inviolable? Or does it shift based on its framing, what is seen and what is unseen? What does a painting of Emmett Till in his casket need to show us?

Historian Martin Berger has written in *Seeing Through Race* of how white media of the 1960s suppressed the circulation of the image of Till in his casket. "Given the importance of the Till murder to the history of civil rights, and the absence of visual representations of the boy's suffering in the white press," writes Berger, "analysis of the coverage of his death provides insights into the complex symbolic work that black children performed in the white imagination." For Berger, "the modern civil rights movement was grounded on the unrepresented body of a black child," namely Till, whose absence from the covers of mainstream newspapers indicated that "the idea of suffering black children was of greater interest to whites than visual evidence of their plight."[1] Berger argues that white progressives' inability to see Till as both a child and a visual manifestation of the everyday horror of white supremacy has hobbled efforts to improve social conditions for African Americans since the Civil Rights Era. His point is underscored by the similar rhetoric employed around the 2014 death of Michael Brown in Ferguson, Missouri, nearly sixty years later. In both cases, Black youths were described as "men," their physical and sexual maturity greatly exaggerated, as a means of engendering public sympathy for the white men who committed the acts of killing.

In an interview with *artnet*, Schutz defended her painting: "It was the feeling of understanding and sharing the pain, the horror"[2] that she sought to capture with *Open Casket*. In the *New*

York Times, she said, "My engagement with this image was through empathy with his mother."[3] Again to *artnet*: "I could never, ever know her experience, but I know what it is to love your child." From Schutz's perspective as a white woman, her recognition of Till as a child deserving of a mother's care is a radical rethinking of the traditional relationship between white female and Black male. Disinclined to identify with Till's accuser, Carolyn Bryant, Schutz speaks of feeling such empathy for the young Black men murdered in contemporary America that it prompts her to imagine herself as Mamie Till Bradley. Her painting—a methodical exercise of studying Till's mutilated face and caressing it into existence through the slow buildup of paint—demonstrates the limits of that empathy as a tool for connection. Berger again: "When a focus on the innocent and helpless precludes attention to and sympathy for the politically active and strong, then sympathy for kids becomes part of the racial problem [...] In highlighting white concern for Till or the children of the Birmingham campaign, we risk overlooking the significant limitations of white empathy."[4] Here Schutz can see only herself, imagining the experience of joy and pain that is Black motherhood. She cannot see the truth of what she imagines, so enamored is she of her own capacity to empathize. Schutz to *artnet*: "I always had issues with making this painting, everything about it. And it is still uncertain for me." What artist of color would dare to put a work so unresolved on public display, let alone be invited to do so in a major museum? What artist of color would have so little to say and yet stand so firm in her assertion that she ought to speak, and be heard?

Some critics of the painting have faulted the Biennial's curators, Christopher Y. Lew and Mia Locks, for racial insensitivity in including this work. It is an ironic charge for two Asian American curators, who for the first time lead the Biennial team without a white colleague. Is it a tone-deaf choice? Possibly. Is it intended to foreclose dialogue around race, or to provoke it? Speaking to *artnet*, Lew described his intention to address questions of race head-on in the exhibition: "We spend our everyday lives skirting around these issues, but they're really built into the show—we're not running away from these discussions."[5] Asian Americans, though hardly a homogenous group or evenly represented in the art world, frequently find themselves awash in racial nuance when debates turn black-and-white.

Even the controversial call to destroy Schutz's painting, issued by artist Hannah Black in an open letter,[6] is anticipated in the Biennial. The presentation of Frances Stark's paintings, which employ text appropriated from the writings of musician Ian Svenonius, constitutes a vigorous defense of censorship on grounds of its necessity in equalizing political representation in cultural spaces, much as Black suggests. One wonders whether Black, a Berlin-based artist of Black and Jewish heritage, saw *Open Casket* in its 2016 debut at Contemporary Fine Arts, in Berlin, as Lew did, and whether the work could have been read differently there given Schutz's own Jewish background. What role Schutz's painting was intended to play in the Biennial's racial dialogue is unclear, although it represents the lone instance of a white artist attempting to wrestle directly with questions of race. If the curators thought they would balance the scales by including *Open Casket*, thereby showing that white artists were open to engagement with racial issues, they blundered by neglecting to recognize that a white artist's engagement must be with the racial imaginary of whiteness in order to matter. That complicated and ugly construct is one that few Americans of any race are well equipped to dismantle.

What does a painting of Emmett Till in his casket need to show us? How racial violence is a socialized, not an anti-social, behavior pattern for whites. How the dismembered must be put together into perfect victims or else their bodily integrity is inferred to have been provisional, if they were ever endowed with that integrity to begin with. "Abjection" is shorthand for how the parts of a Black body never quite resolve into a human view. Schutz's painting would have to explore the uncanny, where like and unlike collide in a deeply unsettling way. She would have to position herself deliberately, not as a casual spectator at Till's funeral, but as a purposeful witness. She would have to make explicit the task of allowing Till to be a *child*—not a man, not a monster, and not a symbol. To be uncertain about racial violence is a privilege. To be affronted by racial violence is a human imperative. Schutz pulls her punches in *Open Casket*. Too gentle to reenact the violence of Till's murder with her brush, she shows us instead what it is like to look endlessly and still never truly see.

1   Berger, *Seeing through Race: A Reinterpretation of Civil Rights Photography*, 126.

2   Boucher, "Dana Schutz Responds to the Uproar Over Her Emmett Till Painting at the Whitney Biennial," *artnet*.

3   Kennedy, "White Artist's Painting of Emmett Till at Whitney Biennial Draws Protests," *New York Times*.

4   Berger, *Seeing through Race*, 140.

5   Goldstein, "Why Dana Schutz's Emmett Till Painting Must Stay," *artnet*.

6   Hannah Black writes: "Through his mother's courage, Till was made available to Black people as an inspiration and warning. Non-Black people must accept that they will never embody and cannot understand this gesture: the evidence of their collective lack of understanding is that Black people go on dying at the hands of white supremacists, that Black communities go on living in desperate poverty not far from the museum where this valuable painting hangs, that Black children are still denied childhood. Even if Schutz has not been gifted with any real sensitivity to history, if Black people are telling her that the painting has caused unnecessary hurt, she and you must accept the truth of this. The painting must go." See: Greenberger, "'The Painting Must Go': Hannah Black Pens Open Letter to the Whitney About Controversial Biennial Work," *ARTnews*.

Conceptualizing Difference

A March 2015 performance at Brown University by conceptual poet Kenneth Goldsmith has resurrected what had seemed to be a long-ago-settled debate. Goldsmith, whose poetic practice is based on appropriation, presented an adaptation of the autopsy report of Ferguson, Missouri, police shooting victim Michael Brown[1] as a poetic reading during the *Interrupt 3* arts festival. The subsequent commentary has largely taken Goldsmith to task for what many perceive as a tasteless and implicitly racist work of art.[2] As collateral damage, many of Goldsmith's critics have been quick to dismiss the validity of conceptual or appropriation strategies as legitimate art practice, despite such forms having firmly established precedents throughout the past century. Furthermore, some have suggested that conceptualism is a mode of artistic practice that serves to reinforce white supremacy.

To what degree are these claims valid, and does Goldsmith's effort have any legitimacy? From an emotional perspective, as a person of color in the United States, it is difficult not to take umbrage at the image of a white man, a published poet and Ivy League academic, appropriating the murdered body of a Black man for the benefit of a largely white audience that may be sympathetic but cannot empathize with the deceased. However, emotion is hardly the most productive filter through which to perceive conceptual art. Deliberately affectless, many conceptual strategies hinge on re-presentation rather than representation, and "treatment" rather than interpretation. Artistically, Goldsmith's biggest failure is that he violates the tenets of conceptualism that dictate a text be either appropriated whole or subjected to a chance-based rather than choice-based editing process. Goldsmith does neither; instead he cherry-picks sections and replaces clinical terms with more digestible ones. Many of Goldsmith's critics have called out his decision to end his reading at a description of the murdered Brown's genitals, truncating the original report in order to close on a salacious detail that evokes memories of lynchings and castrations in the collective racial consciousness.

These alterations appear designed to engage the audience emotionally—a goal antithetical to most conceptual artists, who typically aim for detachment. Goldsmith himself coedited the anthology *Against Expression*, a collection of "conceptual writing," to represent this kind of approach, so one would assume he understands the tenets. Why, then, violate the code of re-presentation in the treatment of this particular document? The more extreme among Goldsmith's critics have argued that this is evidence of his support for a white supremacist culture, but more moderate voices acknowledge that it is more likely a case of implicit bias. Social-justice scholar Dr. Robin DiAngelo has coined the term "white fragility"[3] to describe a phenomenon whereby white individuals who are conscious of racism and motivated by good intentions nonetheless impose themselves within a dialogue on race in overbearing ways, so threatened is their sense of centrality by a discourse that does not rely on them to exist. This concept helps to explain why Goldsmith, an advocate of appropriation without intervention, would be unable to treat the Brown autopsy without imposing his own voice, in violation of conceptualist ethics.

What, then, of the charge that conceptualism itself is an artistic strategy that promotes white supremacy? One might be excused for believing it if "conceptual art" is defined by the overwhelmingly white and male canon of American artists lionized by institutions such as the Museum of Modern Art over the past several decades. On the other hand, prominent scholars including Thomas McEvilley and Terry Smith have identified a non-Western philosophical basis for the synthesis of idea and form that we have come to call conceptualism. For example, McEvilley articulates how conceptual formalism deviates from Cartesian mind-body duality, acknowledging the Buddhist doctrine of *abhidharma* that posits the mind as a sensing, as well as a thinking, organ.[4] This strain of thought gives rise to the Romantic philosophers, with their abiding interest in phenomenology, a means of understanding through experience above comprehension. Smith acknowledges how avant-garde ideas that permeated the West in the 1960s can be found in contemporary art from Japan as early as the 1950s.[5] Although the proto-conceptual breakthrough period in Japan was short-lived, artists who witnessed these developments, including Nam June Paik, Yoko Ono, On Kawara, and Shigeko Kubota, were instrumental in their advancement in Europe and the United States in the following decades. A similar case has been made for proto-conceptual artists working in Latin America in the early 1960s.

Perhaps even more persuasive than these historical arguments are the words of artist Charles Gaines, whose work since the early 1970s has applied conceptual art strategies to an ongoing consideration of the implicit codes of seeing and differentiating that underpin our race-conscious society. Gaines was the subject of a 2014–15 historical survey, *Gridwork (1974-1989)*, organized by the Studio Museum in Harlem and traveling to the Hammer Museum, in Los Angeles. In a letter to leading conceptual artist and mentor Sol LeWitt, cited in the exhibition's wall text, Gaines explains: "I use color not as an affective gesture, but as a code to establish difference." Gaines addresses race in his work subtly, through abstracted, affectless, yet no less potent means.

Gaines devises systems designed to remove his artistic process from conscious choice such that self-expression is elided in favor of a more objective outcome. Discussing his work with artist Sam Durant at the Hammer earlier this month, Gaines explained that his practice is a struggle against "art as a subjective practice," and that he seeks to avoid aesthetic decision-making because it privileges "the idea of beauty or pleasure as emerging from the site of the self or the ego." Abandoning these Western values based in individualism and hierarchy, Gaines further described how his epiphany occurred when he turned away from the Western canon as a young man and began to investigate Muslim and Buddhist traditions of artistic practice, in which individual expression and emotional affect were secondary to systematic, mathematically derived formal investigations. This breakthrough was, in Gaines's words, a means of responding to the "influence of non-Western ideas

#APPROPRIATION   #ACCESS   #CONCEPTUALISM   #RACE   #INSTITUTIONS

but […] to think about them within the language I have competency in." Conceptualism here becomes a strategy for critiquing white supremacy, albeit one that differs significantly from the overtly racialized representational art of Gaines's peers in the Black Arts Movement of the 1960s and 1970s.

While artists of color have played a substantial role in the advancement of conceptual art from its origins until the present day, it remains the case that the institutional framework for art is defined by the values of racial hierarchy. As Robin DiAngelo explains, white Euro Americans "have organized society to reproduce and reinforce our racial interests and perspectives." As such, there can be no neutral territory for an institutionalized presentation on questions of race and racism, as in the case of Goldsmith's reading. Host institution Brown University has historical connections to the Trans-Atlantic slave trade and represents the intellectual and material wealth of a nation that was built on the forced labor of a Black underclass. In this context, the spectacle of a white poet presenting the murdered body of a Black man cannot be assumed to be affectless or dispassionate. DiAngelo advises that white allies seeking to improve their comprehension of racially fraught subjects attempt "to understand the racial realities of people of color through authentic interaction rather than through the media or unequal relationships" and to take "action to address our own racism, the racism of other whites, and the racism embedded in our institutions."[6] Goldsmith may genuinely have believed that by reading his poem he was doing the latter: forcing a white audience in a white institutional context to acknowledge the horror of police brutality committed daily against Black men. Unfortunately his inability to do the former—to seek understanding through authentic interaction rather than a mediated, unequal relationship—appears to have been his undoing. DiAngelo correctly points out that racial discrimination is maintained through social systems rather than individual actions. We would be remiss to allow Goldsmith's highly public failure to dissuade us from using systems-based art and theory as tools to dismantle structures of oppression.

1   For future posterity: Eighteen-year-old Michael Brown was shot August 9, 2014, in Ferguson, Missouri, by white police officer Darren Wilson after Brown was accused of robbing a convenience store. Wilson was not indicted.

2   Rin Johnson, an artist in the audience of Goldsmith's reading, writes: "To take a document like this and attempt to make it into a form of art is blatantly not engaging with the issues at hand. Using a white body to try to interpret and illustrate the violence wrought upon black bodies in America is lazy." See: Johnson, "On Hearing a White Man Co-opt the Body of Michael Brown," *Hyperallergic*.

3   DiAngelo, "White Fragility: Why It's So Hard to Talk to White People About Racism," *The Good Men Project*.

4   McEvilley, *The Triumph of Anti-Art*, 79.

5   Smith, *Contemporary Art: World Currents*, 20.

6   DiAngelo, "White Fragility."

Toward the Black Museum

The recent controversy over Kelley Walker's exhibition *Direct Drive* (2016) at the Contemporary Art Museum St. Louis, and the subsequent resignation of that exhibition's curator, Jeffrey Uslip, were more reminders that museums are not built and programmed for all audiences alike. As this column has taken up questions of race in the museum on numerous occasions (and class in the museum, and gender in the museum), a comment on the St. Louis situation seems warranted. Public protests were mounted after audiences discovered that Walker's artwork consisted of enlarged, appropriated photos of African Americans, smeared with toothpaste. Against the backdrop of outcries precipitated by the killing of Michael Brown in nearby Ferguson, the decision to feature a white, New York–based artist whose work takes up race in a manner that is provocative but not analytical seems almost comically ham-fisted. Still, both Uslip and CAM's director, Lisa Melandri, have steadfastly defended the artist and the exhibition despite the artist's apparent failure to articulate any coherent justification or motivation for his work.

Some observers are scratching their heads, wondering how this public-relations train-wreck could have been avoided. Others contend that racially insensitive missteps such as these are inevitable when the leadership of art museums across the country remains largely a hermetically sealed echo chamber of apologetic, but unshakeable, whiteness.[1] Simone Leigh's installation (2016–2017) in the Hammer Museum's Hammer Projects series proposes an alternative to the typically white, upper-middle-class hegemony of the contemporary art gallery or museum. The central structure within her exhibition is *Cupboard IV* (2016), a round hut made of raffia and stoneware that references the forms and materials of sub-Saharan architectures built predominantly by women. The hut is an early indicator that Leigh's exhibition is shifting our notions of the "default" contemporary art viewer. Within the structure, a video plays of independent curator and choreographer Rashida

Bumbray, dressed to the nines in a floor-length gold lamé gown, dancing furiously with bells around her ankles. The elegance, power, and grace of her body contrast with a mounting sense of exhaustion and futility as the performance goes on.

On an adjacent wall of the gallery, five sculptures from Leigh's series *Anatomy of Architecture* (2016) passively adorn the exhibition space, bearing silent witness. Four of these are recognizable as sculptural busts, glazed deep black, with recognizably African American features. Their heads are crowned with dozens of tiny, colorful ceramic flowers. A fifth sculpture, second from the right, offers only a gaping void where a head or face would be. The effect is silencing, and violent. Delicacy and decoration contrast with erasure—the two polarities of the female condition. This work extends bell hooks's concept of "an aesthetic of Blackness" beyond the home and private sphere and into institutional space. In "An Aesthetic of Blackness: Strange and Oppositional," hooks writes:

> *In one house I learned the place of aesthetics in the lives of agrarian poor black folks. There the lesson was that one had to understand beauty as a force to be made and imagined. Old folks shared their sense that we had come out of slavery into this free space and we had to create a world that would renew the spirit, that would make it life-giving. In that house there was a sense of history. In the other house, the one I lived in, aesthetics had no place. There the lessons were never about art or beauty, but always only to possess things.*[2]

If the museum is the repository of our collective historical aesthetic, the actions of the CAM staff suggest that engagement with the institution's African American neighbors was more about possession—of the narrative, of the moral high ground, of decision-making—than it was about "life-giving."[3]

Continues hooks: "Critical theories about cultural production, about aesthetics, continue to confine and restrict black artists, and passive withdrawal from a discussion of aesthetics is a useless response [...] Black artists concerned with producing work that embodies and reflects a liberatory politic know that an important part of any decolonization process is critical intervention and interrogation of existing repressive and dominating structures."[4] While Walker employs the rhetoric of "anti-aesthetic" in lieu of cogent social or political critique, Black artists do not have this luxury. Craft, technique, and awareness of the history of materials are very much evident in Leigh's work, which takes up subjects cast as inherently abject by the cultural mainstream for their unapologetic Blackness but appeals on a technical and material level to curators and audiences who might otherwise marginalize the work and its message.

Questions of the body, its commoditization and exchange, are central to this work. African people and their cultural products have been commoditized for over five hundred years, resulting in a worldwide condition of alienation between labor and its outcomes; cultural production is affective, or emotional, labor. Art's continued existence in a fully commoditized society, despite its being undercompensated and undervalued, points to the high intrinsic motivation of artists to produce objects of significance irrespective of whether the culture holds space for them. CAM chose to claim a space for Blackness and then fill it with white guilt. Leigh takes the opposite tack, infusing a space customarily held for white cultural narratives with the boundless energy of Black community-building.

1   Writing in *Hyperallergic*, nonprofit director James McAnally suggests that perhaps it is time to admit that "the art world and its institutions are in fact constructed of mutually exclusive communities—donors and neighbors, corporate supporters and those seeking alternatives, the 'diverse' demographics claimed in a grant report and those whom the exhibitions are actually organized for." See: McAnally, "A Call for a Collective Reexamination of Our Art Institutions," *Hyperallergic*.

2   hooks, "An Aesthetic of Blackness: Strange and Oppositional," *Lenox Avenue: A Journal of Interarts Inquiry*, 66.

3   For a more complete recap of the actions (and inaction) of the CAM staff in regards to Walker's exhibition, see: *Artforum*, "Director of Contemporary Art Museum St. Louis Responds to Critics of Decision to Wall Off Kelley Walker Exhibition."

4   hooks, "An Aesthetic of Blackness: Strange and Oppositional," 69–70.

Learn Where the Meat Comes From

With the arrival of the new Whitney Museum of American Art on Gansevoort Street, New York's Meatpacking District completes lower Manhattan's transition from a no-man's-land populated by artists and outcasts to a stomping ground for fashionable elites. Befitting of an institution that represents the American art world—which has long positioned itself within both these groups, often simultaneously—the Whitney would seem to want to have it both ways. With the museum's inaugural exhibition, *America Is Hard to See* (2015), audiences are presented with a chronological reworking of the history of American art as collected by the Whitney. The works installed on five floors of the gleaming Renzo Piano building tell a story that is complex, and at times contradictory, while demonstrating the limitations of official art-historical narratives in articulating the various trajectories of art and culture in the United States and in the twentieth century.

The good news is that Whitney curators, led by chief curator and deputy director for programs Donna De Salvo, have systematically sought out gaps in the museum's permanent collection and attempted to fill in missing contributors to American art history since the late nineteenth century, with particular attention paid to works by women and people of color. Less encouraging is the limited impact that these new introductions have had on the curatorial framing of American art's influences and objectives. On the eighth floor, covering the years 1910 to 1940, unfamiliar names like Nancy Elizabeth Prophet and Richmond Barthé, both African American sculptors associated with the Harlem Renaissance, join a familiar roster that includes Marsden Hartley, Joseph Stella, Lyonel Feininger, Georgia O'Keeffe, and Isamu Noguchi. The historical narrative is expanded a bit to include African and Asian influences as well as European modernism. Yet non-Western influences are cited only in discussions of the works by artists of color, while the overarching themes of industrialization and geometric abstraction as American art's primary interests in that period are preserved from earlier presentations of the collection. An opportunity to connect American modernism writ large to the United States' emergence as a global power is thereby wholly missed.

On the seventh floor, covering the years 1925 to 1960, images of immigration and alienation in the cities from artists including Charles White, Maya Deren, and George Tooker begin to compete with heroic depictions of the American West by Andrew Wyeth, Grant Wood, and Chiura Obata (whose *ukiyo-e* woodblock prints of America's national parks represent a major recent acquisition and a collection highlight). These themes converge in the work of Edward Hopper, who blends the clear light and detail of the landscape genre with the psychological charge of Surrealism. Mannerism—an aesthetic of exaggerated natural forms to achieve a sense of artificiality and asymmetry—appears as a tool of social critique in works by Thomas Hart Benton, Reginald Marsh, and Paul Cadmus, which in turn invoke the caricatures of German Expressionists George Grosz and Otto Dix, though that relationship is not articulated at the museum. Social Realists working in printmaking and photography, including Mabel Dwight, Hugo Gellert, Margaret Bourke-White, Lisette Model, Walker Evans, and Weegee, depict the era as tumultuous and divided: plagued by poverty, labor abuses, racist violence, and war. A suite of important paintings by Jacob Lawrence, *War Series* (1946–47), and a major work by Ben Shahn, *The Passion of Sacco and Vanzetti* (1931–32), situate these themes within a larger historical sweep. Sited somewhat incongruously at the center of this storm of passion and rage is Alexander Calder's whimsical Calder's *Circus* (1926–31)—one of the Whitney's best-loved works—embodying the energy but not the anxiety of the works in its vicinity.

That combination of energy and anxiety continues, although stripped of historical specificity, in the adjacent gallery of Abstract Expressionism including works by Arshile Gorky, Willem de Kooning, Philip Guston, Alfonso Ossorio, Alma Thomas, and Joan Mitchell. While some artists such as Gorky and Guston can be said to have been responding to social upheaval and ethnic violence, the historical engagement of the Social Realists has been replaced by introspection and metaphor. Abstract Expressionism's reputation for large-scale machismo is beautifully challenged by the central placement of Lee Krasner's *The Seasons* (1957), a work nearly seventeen-by-eight feet that is rambunctious and pastoral at once. Painted shortly after the death of Krasner's husband, Jackson Pollock, *The Seasons* shows Krasner coming into her own as both a major painter and a woman who no longer fears the critics' dismissive characterizations of her work as "feminine." Complemented with sculptures by Louise Bourgeois and Ruth Asawa, this arrangement balances the traditional masculine narrative of the period with female points of view.

The sixth floor, including works from 1950 to 1975, fluctuates between the serenity of geometric abstraction and the clamor of assemblage. A tranquil, meditative tenor is established by paintings from Agnes Martin, Ad Reinhardt, Ellsworth Kelly, Frank Stella, Jo Baer, Carmen Herrera, and Jasper Johns, only to be radically disrupted by the reentry of day-to-day life into art's refined spaces. Arguably the strongest grouping in the whole museum brings New York art stars like Robert Rauschenberg, Claes Oldenburg, John Chamberlain, and Ray Johnson into dialogue with West Coast artists such as Noah Purifoy, Jay DeFeo, Bruce Conner, Wallace Berman, (Marjorie) Cameron, and Jess (Collins). Artists of color including Raphael Montañez Ortiz and women including Lee Bontecou are given pride of place, effecting a balance of perspectives as with the Abstract Expressionist gallery above. These groupings are rewarding because they respond to diversity without reducing the curatorial narrative to a lecture on diversity—allowing each artist to function as an artist, engaged with form and material, and equally entitled to ambiguity and open-ended interpretation.

This openness and inclusion is maintained throughout the sixth floor, with works by Yayoi Kusama, Marisol (Escobar), Malcolm Bailey, Lee Lozano, Nam June Paik, and Betye Saar alongside Andy Warhol, James Rosenquist, Ed Ruscha, and

Wayne Thiebaud. Regrettably, these works from the 1960s and early 1970s are the last in painting and sculpture to challenge official narratives within the exhibition as a whole. A gallery dedicated to Minimalism includes Rafael Ferrer, Eva Hesse, Anne Truitt, and Michelle Stuart but subverts these artists' contributions to an established discourse centered on Donald Judd and Richard Serra, who dominate the space. On the fifth floor, covering 1965 to the present, a terrific collection of videos approaches gender, racial, and geographic parity by linking the interests of Suzanne Lacy, Eleanor Antin, Lynda Benglis, Hermine Freed, Cynthia Maughan, Howardena Pindell, and Ulysses Jenkins with more frequently shown works by Vito Acconci, Chris Burden, Paul McCarthy, Martha Rosler, Joan Jonas, and William Wegman. Feminism is very much on display in video and photography by many of these artists as well as Hannah Wilke, Dara Birnbaum, Laurie Simmons, and Adrian Piper. However, with the exception of Lacy, artists representing the Feminist Art Program and the Woman's Building that emerged from Los Angeles in the 1970s are absent.

In works from the 1980s through the present, the influence of the contemporary art market seems to inform selections in painting and sculpture as much as, or more than, the interests of posterity. Works by Jean-Michel Basquiat, Kara Walker, Mark Bradford, David Hammons, and Jimmie Durham do less to challenge the official narrative than to demonstrate how contemporary art frameworks have adapted to incorporate artists of color and social-justice themes within a thriving luxury-goods economy over the past forty years. This is not to say that the work is weak. Basquiat's *Hollywood Africans* (1983) is to the Whitney what Picasso's *Demoiselles d'Avignon* (1907) is to the MoMA collection: a watershed. Martin Wong's *Big Heat* (1986), Mike Kelley's *More Love Hours Than Can Ever Be Repaid and the Wages of Sin* (1987), Fred Wilson's *Guarded View* (1991), and Catherine Opie's *Self-Portrait/Cutting* (1993) will likewise be recognized by future generations as significant points of departure. Still, these works operate less like counterpoints to an official narrative than as its reinforcements, as the story has shifted from one of America's heroic, masculine exceptionalism to one of America's heartfelt yet superficial remorse at the inequality and pain we would prefer to believe we have left in the past.

Two works best encapsulate the conflict at the heart of the new Whitney Museum: Hans Haacke's *Shapolsky et al. Manhattan Real Estate Holdings, a Real-Time Social System, as of May 1, 1971* (1971) and Karen Kilimnik's *The Hellfire Club Episode of the Avengers* (1989). Haacke turns his critical eye on real-estate transactions in lower Manhattan, chronicling exploitation of dire economic conditions by the wealthy to profit from the displacement of working-class New Yorkers. His work hangs in a gallery inside a $422 million building atop a natural-gas pipeline on a street that, in 1971, was home to slaughterhouses and transgender sex workers, and today hosts exclusive restaurants and a Louboutin store. Kilimnik's installation considers a 1966 episode of the British serial *The Avengers*, "A Touch of Brimstone," in which the titular spies infiltrate a fictional BDSM club that shares a name with one of the now defunct sex clubs of Gansevoort Street circa 1980—90. Banned from broadcast in the United States, the episode represents how popular media both absorbs and defangs what was once underground. Perhaps few people would begrudge the glittering river views of the new Whitney building for the AIDS-related anxiety and crushing poverty experienced by New York's LGBTQI community between the late 1970s and the mid-1990s. Nonetheless, the disappearance of that history from the shiny new Meatpacking District comes with an unaccounted-for cost. As Suzanne Lacy admonishes us, it's important to "learn where the meat comes from."[1]

1   Suzanne Lacy's *Learn Where the Meat Comes From* (1976), a photographic series and performance created for video, features the artist situated in a telegenic kitchen wrestling a cut of meat into submission. In it, she instructs: "Innumerable housewives buy lamb year after year, often spending hundreds of dollars […] Taking the time to learn where the meat comes from will ensure your constant success […] If you're willing to make yourself utterly ridiculous, you can learn the different cuts in just a few minutes." See: http://www.suzannelacy.com/learn-where-the-meat-comes-from/.

#GENTRIFICATION #HISTORICITY #MARKETS #COLLECTIONS #ACCESS #MUSEUMS

On Disgust

An act of senseless violence[1] at UC Santa Barbara has re-ignited an online conversation about the interrelationship between race, gender, discrimination, and violence. While the tweets and subsequent articles around #yesallwomen[2] have drawn public attention to the gendered assumptions that underpin violent behavior, less visibility has accrued to the role that Orientalism played in dehumanizing and desexualizing both the perpetrator and the victims of the attack that left seven young adults dead on May 23, 2014. My interest here is not to revisit the particulars of the crime or to give the killer any more attention. Instead, I will use the productive conversations that have emerged from this horrid tragedy to consider how we are "socialized to reject," as artist Rina Banerjee puts it in the context of her current solo exhibition, *Disgust* (2014), at LA Louver.

The effect of Banerjee's installation of assemblage sculptures and small, surreal paintings is far from disgusting; rather, the works possess a strange and alien beauty. This dual attraction-revulsion is reflective of how both misogyny and Orientalism operate by simultaneously idealizing and dehumanizing the human object of acquisitive desire. Artists may experience a similar condition in the marketplace, which functions by idealizing their creative energies as "genius" while devaluing the labor they put into creating their work.

Banerjee makes her sculptures from a mix of organic and industrially fabricated materials, including molded polymers, shells, bones, ceramics, wire, and feathers. They often appear as uncanny, lifelike beings wielding lengthy poetic passages in place of titles. An elephantine figure draped in red taffeta and emblazoned with cowrie shells and ceramic eyes is titled *She was now in western style dress covered in part of Empires' ruffle and red dress, had a foreign and peculiar race, a Ganesha who had lost her head, was thrown across sea until herself shipwrecked. A native of Bangladesh lost foot to root in Videsh, followed her mother full stop on forehead, trapped tongue of horn and grew ram-like under stress* (2011). This effigy reflects the conflicted, fragmented, and dehumanized nature of the transcultural condition experienced by Banerjee, whose dual Indian and Bengali identifications represent a split identity that does not easily reconcile to Western expectations of immigrants' cultural authenticity. "Videsh," or foreign trade, corrupts the deity "Ganesha," strips her of her intellect, wrecks her capacity for self-expression, and ultimately transforms the playful elephant into a stubborn, aggressive ram.

In a video produced by the gallery, Banerjee articulates this experience of difference in the context of "disgust" as "a way of thinking about what is so clear in our emotional response that it forms a boundary." Her works explore the emotional ramifications of our expectations of normalcy and difference, which in extreme cases can trigger acts of extremism and aggression in unstable individuals, as we saw in Santa Barbara. While dramatic acts of aggression make headlines, far more common are a litany of daily micro-aggressions that represent a "death by a thousand cuts" inflicted upon the self-esteem of many who identify as culturally hybrid. Neither authentically "other" nor comfortably "us," hybrid identity—often interracial, but also transcultural—disproves binary ideas of difference. The struggle between "self" and "other" becomes an internal one that is simultaneously writ large on the culture as a whole.

Banerjee describes her mixed-media painting *Dressmaker and Shopping girl: Chinese goods and garment Industry tinsel, made in Hong Kong, made in India for export from port to port made by small hands and little hands, short people from far away lands. Dressmaker ghost follows me around from shop to shop in Big country with large people with Big hands and high heels* (2014) as a depiction of "experiencing yourself to the point of vanity in that kind of greed that women are accused of." In this work, beauty is itself a source of disgust. Socially conditioned toward superficial and acquisitive values, the ideal young woman must walk a fine line between adornment and self-aggrandizement in order to remain within propriety's bounds. Her beauty must always be intended for the consumption of others. Any manifestation of her own desires—to be admired, desired, autonomous—is a transgression and a trigger for disgust, or even violence.

Banerjee is clear that disgust, while subconsciously triggered, is not an innate response but a socialized one. She is interested in how social cues "train us to be disgusted" by different bodies, different ideas, and different ways of being. In the case of the Santa Barbara murders, the perpetrator prefaced his rampage by articulating desire and disgust around his own mixed-race body as well as the bodies of those he identified as racially and/or sexually "other." His aggression was framed as a bulwark against emasculation, bound up in racialization, rejection, and an expectation of white privilege by birthright that was only halfway his. Half-white and half-Asian, he was tormented by an internal conflict that was a vicious distortion of the struggle that hapa-identified Americans often experience with respect to reconciling their own identification as both colonizer and colonized. Rina Banerjee's work represents a better way forward in our negotiation of these common complexities, as she asks us to confront and negotiate our own capacity for disgust and for compassion.

1   On May 23, 2014, 22-year-old Elliot Rodger killed six people and injured fourteen others near University of California, Santa Barbara, before killing himself.

2   Following the Isla Vista killings, women began using the #yesallwomen hashtag on Twitter to share their personal stories of sexual assault and abuse.

#HYBRIDITY   #ORIENTALISM   #RACISM   #MISOGYNY   #VIOLENCE   #OTHER

The Body Without Organs

Given their constant presence in our lives, we think surprisingly
little about our bodies. When we do, we are often thinking of
ways to make them less body, more commodity. For women in
particular, the body is the site of our social acceptability and our
abjection. Fashion is how we navigate that landscape. Philosopher
Kwame Anthony Appiah has proposed that the true challenge
of the present cosmopolitan landscape, in which many disparate
groups must adjust to living together, is not in navigating
"difference" but in negotiating disagreements around the relative importance of a set of values in relation to one another:
"Even if we share a value language, and even if we agree on how
to apply it to a particular case, we can disagree about the
weight to give to different values."[1] If, as described, the prevailing values of fashion idealize and commoditize the female
body, Comme des Garçons designer Rei Kawakubo emphasizes
material and formal investigation, interaction with the body
through movement, and building self-esteem. She takes
this commercial, aesthetic medium and uses it sculpturally,
advancing difficult ideas about beauty, embodiment, and
access. Kawakubo's radical reshuffling of clothing's function,
purpose, and form is the work of an artist, as the Metropolitan
Museum of Art Costume Institute exhibition, *Art of the In-
Between* (2017), demonstrates.

Beauty, for women, is a devil's bargain. Little can be
accomplished without it, given that society values women's
bodies most as decorative objects and least as active agents
of consciousness. Though few women can conform to the
strict social expectations of beauty, all are consistently
encouraged to spend significant resources of money and time
on beauty products, rituals, clothing, and accessories. Enter
Kawakubo, whose creations show that rethinking the values
that traditionally govern fashion and commerce can produce
subversive results. Her clothes operate in the reified realm of
desire as couture objects while making the female body "ugly"
in every way imaginable. They quote copiously, and hilariously,

from the history of aristocratic fashion, annihilating conventions of idealized physical form to instead dwell on the extreme, unexpected, and grotesque. If the expected relationship between the body and fashion requires both to submit to a regime of commodity fetishization, the relationship between the body and Comme des Garçons is one of symbiotic augmentation, two parts that make a greater whole.

Kawakubo gives little weight to the usually prominent values of comfort and flattery. Many of her outfits restrict the body, particularly the arms. A hooded, armless black sweater invokes a massive shroud but also makes the wearer resemble a grade-schooler pulling her head and arms inside her shirt. Jokes about craft are tucked in throughout the show. Billowing gowns are made from materials usually used for blocking and lining, such as craft paper and unbleached cotton ducking. A skirt that looks like an inversion of a suit is mostly cotton ducking with a bit of blue serge wool showing through at the seam. In other collections, layers of richly embroidered and printed fabrics juxtapose contemporary and historical textiles, drapings, and silhouettes. Her infamous 1990s gingham dresses with large tumescent protrusions are featured along with a video of Merce Cunningham's dancers performing *Scenario*, a dance choreographed to be performed in the clothes, in which the dancers' angular movements contrast with the rounded forms.

Shrouding of the head and shoulders is an ongoing interest in Kawakubo's work. The famously private designer invites her wearer to literally disappear into many of her creations. Arms, legs, heads, torsos—these specificities no longer matter. "You never reach the Body without Organs, you can't reach it, you are forever attaining it, it is a limit," say Deleuze and Guattari.[2] The Deleuzian turn in Kawakubo's work resides in her lack of interest in consistency of a conventional sort, either historical or material, while maintaining what the French philosophers called "the *plane of consistency* specific to desire"[3] that characterizes the Body without Organs. Unlike the "organism" that represents an organized system, such as a shirt with one hole for the head and two for the arms, the Body without Organs "constitutes the ontological unity of substance." When a consciousness is fully integrated—when we make ourselves a Body without Organs—the layers or strata that make up a personality such as upbringing, cultural background, race, class, and education can no longer be picked apart and individually analyzed. The internal and external givens of the body, such as limbs, torso, genitals, intestines, lungs, blood, heart, brain, are not experienced by embodied human beings as a collection of discrete parts. The body is an integrated unit, a mind-body totality, moving through the world as a sometimes-incongruous thing that simply is.

The female body is regularly objectified in fashion (as in every other sphere of social relations). Women often forego comfort for beauty, for example wearing towering heels or enduring scorching hair and skin treatments. Deleuze and Guattari: "The masochist's suffering is the price he must pay, not to achieve pleasure, but to untie the pseudo-bond between desire and pleasure as an extrinsic measure."[4] Kawakubo's lack of interest in flattery should not be mistaken for an aversion to sexuality, or to suffering, as some of the clothes render the body alluring in surprising and potentially painful ways. Crucially, desire is decoupled from external validation, freed from the approval or disapproval of others. A bloomer and bondage-straps getup is topped with a Peter Pan collar, recasting Victorian repression and reverence for childhood as a costume for a modern, flirty woman. The history of aesthetics is likewise rewritten to make explicit the imperial violence carried within. In this, her work parallels other forms of popular midcentury Japanese art such as manga, in which restrictive and sexually problematic social mores are rewritten to accommodate liberatory female desire. Bright red "blood" spatters and heaps of black mourning lace, embedded with children's organza dresses, lumps of felt, and massive swaths of fur, all challenge the distinction between organic and inorganic, between living and dead, between a caress and a violation.

Deleuze and Guattari challenge the reader to invent a Body without Organs made of desire and intensity, a social body in which intentionality and self-awareness seamlessly produce new forms of being, disentangled from the imposed order of old histories and old hierarchies. Once you have made yourself over in this way, you are in control of what you embody and what you enact in the world you inhabit. The ideal Body without Organs manifests "immanence," a kind of embodied spirituality that is rooted in the unified self, and can be felt as a powerful energy by others. Kawakubo shows what that ideal Body without Organs might look like. It could be strange, seductive, awkward, and effusive. It might be a dress for two, or a coat that swallows your head. Freedom for the body might even, for the uninitiated, resemble bondage.

1   Appiah, *Cosmopolitanism: Ethics in a World of Strangers.*

2   Deleuze and Guattari, "November 28, 1947: How do you Make Yourself a Body Without Organs?," *A Thousand Plateaus,* 174.

3   Ibid., 179.

4   Ibid., 180.

IMAGES

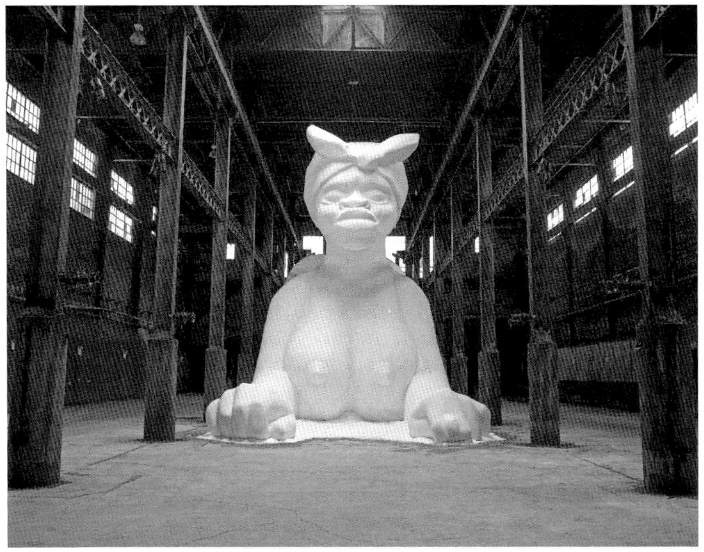

1   **Kara Walker**
At the behest of Creative Time Kara E. Walker has confected: A Subtlety, or the Marvelous Sugar Baby, an Homage to the unpaid and overworked Artisans who have refined our Sweet tastes from the cane fields to the Kitchens of the New World on the Occasion of the demolition of the Domino Sugar Refining Plant, 2014
site-specific installation at Domino Sugar Factory, Brooklyn, NY
Courtesy of Creative Time. Photo: Jason Wyche.

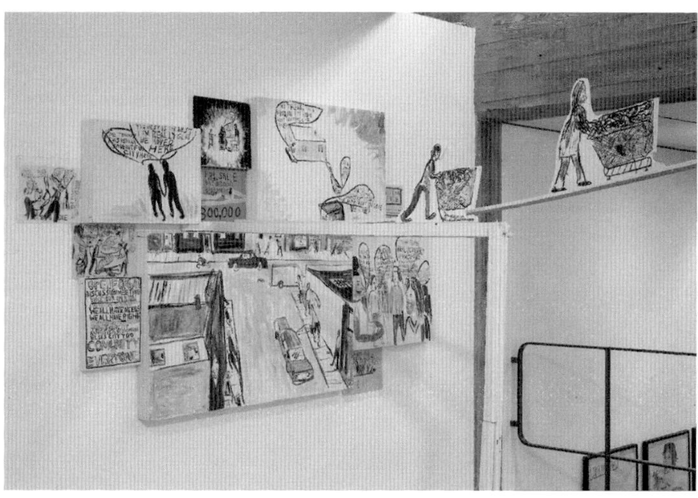

2 **Chris Johanson**
The Survivalists, 1999
installation view, *Energy That Is All Around*, Walter and McBean Galleries,
San Francisco Art Institute, San Francisco, CA, September 12—December 14, 2013
Courtesy of the Artist and Altman Siegal Gallery. Photo: Johnna Arnold/SFAI.

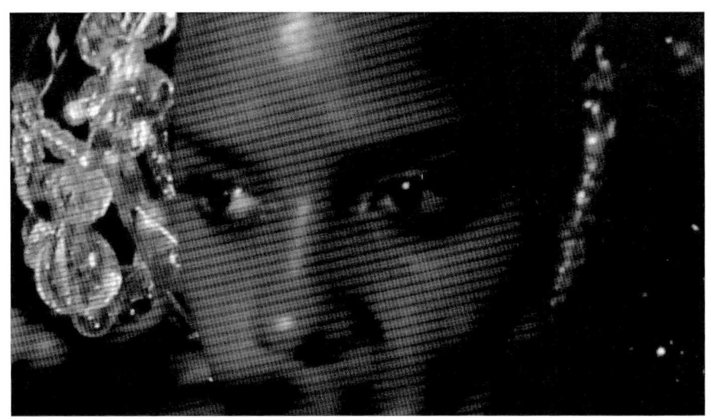

3 **HOWDOYOUSAYYAMINAFRICAN?**
Good Stock on the Dimension Floor: An Opera, 2014
video, color, sound; 54 minutes
Collection of the Artists. © HOWDOYOUSAYYAMINAFRICAN?

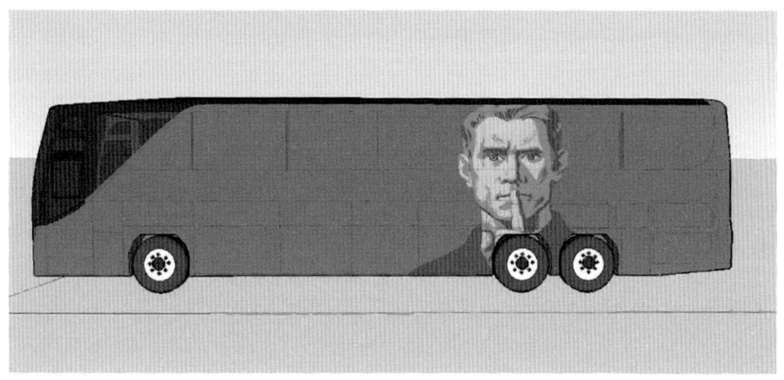

4   **Michal Wisniowski**
"Guard Secrets" Google Bus, 2014
digital image based on **Fangor Wojciech**'s *Strzez tajemnicy panstwowej* (1951)
submission to **Stephanie Syjuco**'s *"Bedazzle a Tech Bus" Call for Entries* (2013)
Courtesy of the Artist.

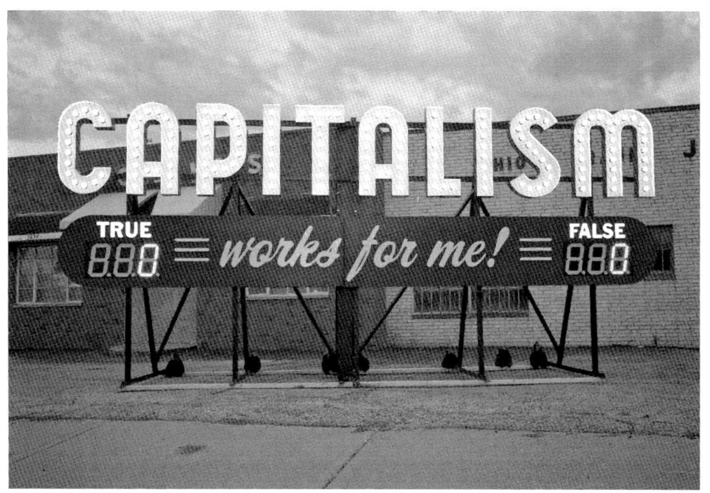

5 **Steve Lambert**

Capitalism Works for Me! True/False, 2011
aluminum and electrical; 9 x 20 x 7 ft.
Courtesy of the Artist and Charlie James Gallery, Los Angeles. CC BY-NC-SA.

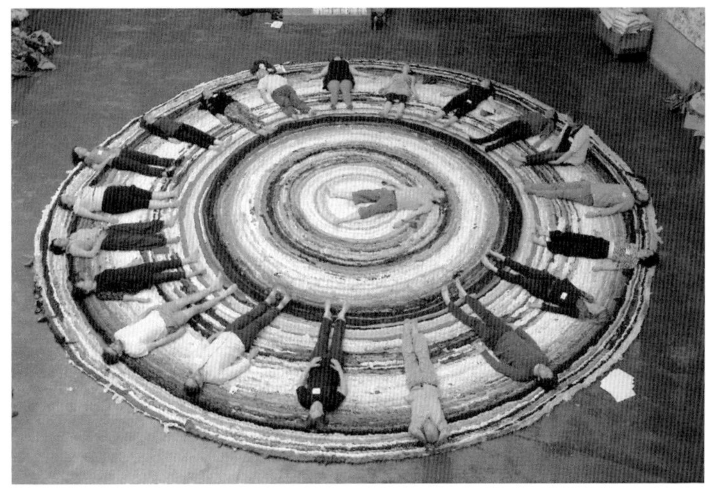

6   **Christian Nagler**, *Yoga for Adjuncts Workshop*, 2014
Fritz Haeg, *Domestic Integrity Field*, 2012–2014 (rug)
On April 19, 2014, the Arts Research Center hosted *Valuing Labor in the Arts: A Practicum*.
This daylong event included a series of artist-led workshops that developed
exercises, prompts, or actions that engage questions of art, labor, and economics.
The workshops took place at the Berkeley Art Museum Pacific Film Archive.
Courtesy of the Arts Research Center, UC Berkeley. Photo: Megan Hoetger.

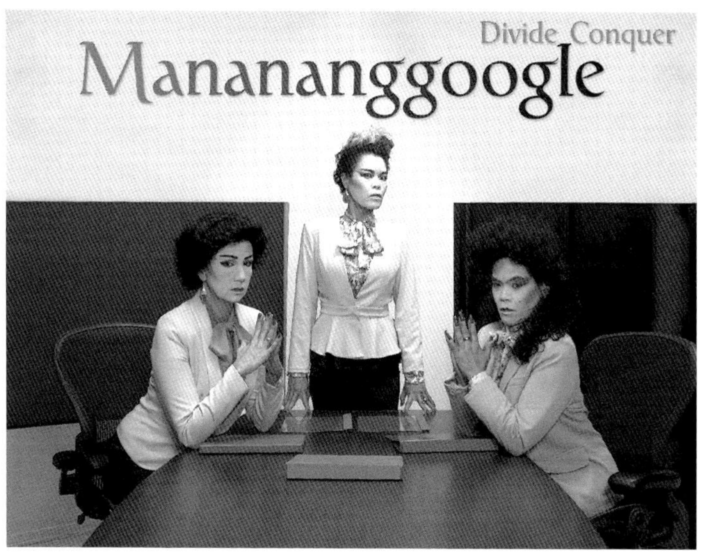

7   **Mail Order Brides/M.O.B. (Jenifer K Wofford, Reanne Estrada, Eliza Barrios)**
Manananggoogle, 2013
multimedia installation including website and photographs
Commissioned by the San Jose Museum of Art with support from The James Irvine
Foundation and MetLife Foundation.

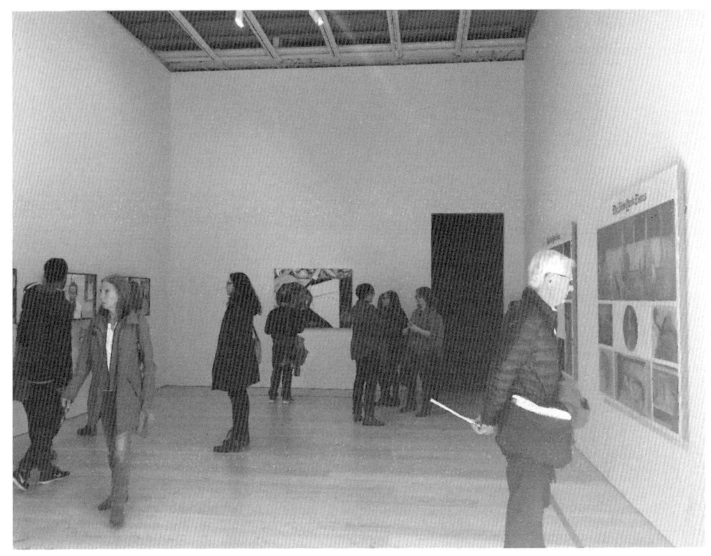

8   **Dana Schutz**, *Open Casket*, 2016 (center)
Maya Stovall, *Liquor Store Theatre*, 2014—2016 (left)
Julian Nguyen, *Executive Function and Executive Solutions*, 2017 (right)
installation view, *Whitney Biennial 2017*, Whitney Museum of American Art,
New York, NY, March 17—June 11, 2017
Schutz: Collection of the Artist.
Stovall: Courtesy of the Artist, Eric Johnston, and Todd Stovall.
Nguyen: Collection of the Artist. Courtesty of Neue Alte Brucke, Frankfurt, and Stuart.
Photo: Anuradha Vikram.

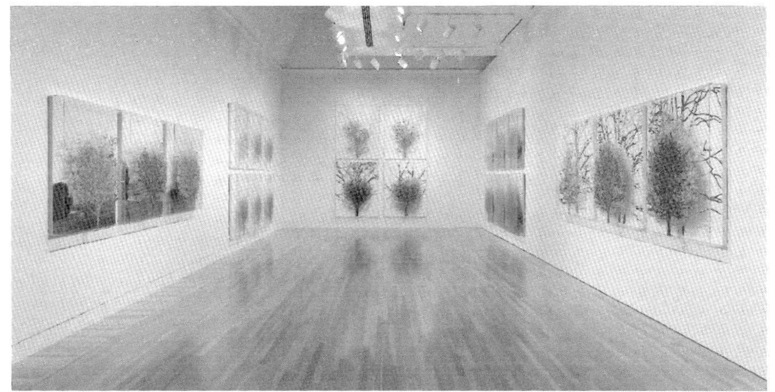

9   **Charles Gaines**
installation view, *Gridwork 1974—1989*, Hammer Museum, Los Angeles, CA,
February 8—May 24, 2015
Courtesy of Hammer Museum. Photo: Brian Forrest.

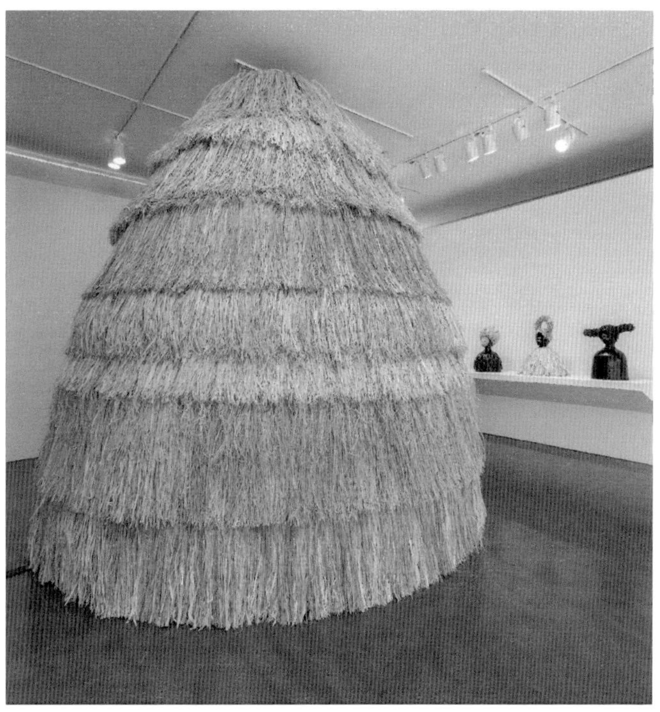

10   **Simone Leigh**
installation view, *Hammer Projects: Simone Leigh*, Hammer Museum, Los Angeles, CA,
September 17, 2016–January 8, 2017
Courtesy of Hammer Museum. Photo: Brian Forrest.

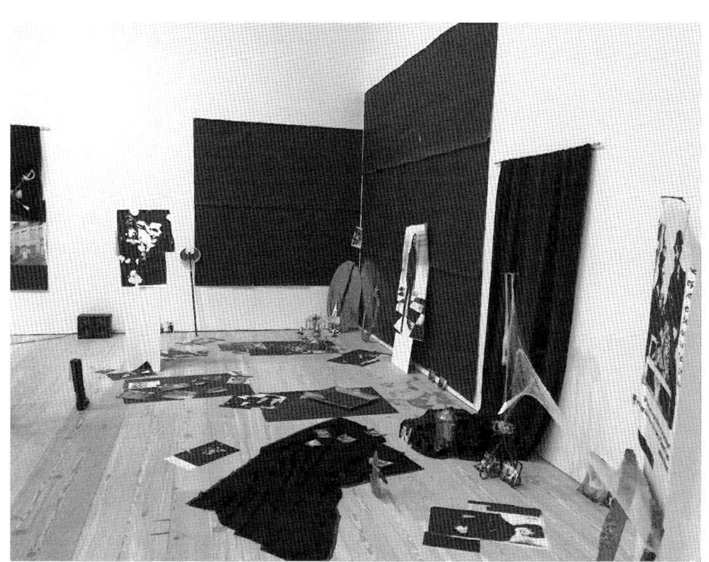

11 **Karen Kilimnik**
The Hellfire Club episode of the Avengers, 1989
fabric, photocopies, candelabra, toy swords, mirror, gilded frames, costume
jewelry, boot, fake cobwebs, silver tankard, audio media player, and dried pea;
dimensions variable
installation view, *America Is Hard to See,* Whitney Museum of American Art, New York, NY,
May 1—September 27, 2015
Gift of Peter M. Brant. Courtesy of the Brant Foundation. Photo: Anuradha Vikram.

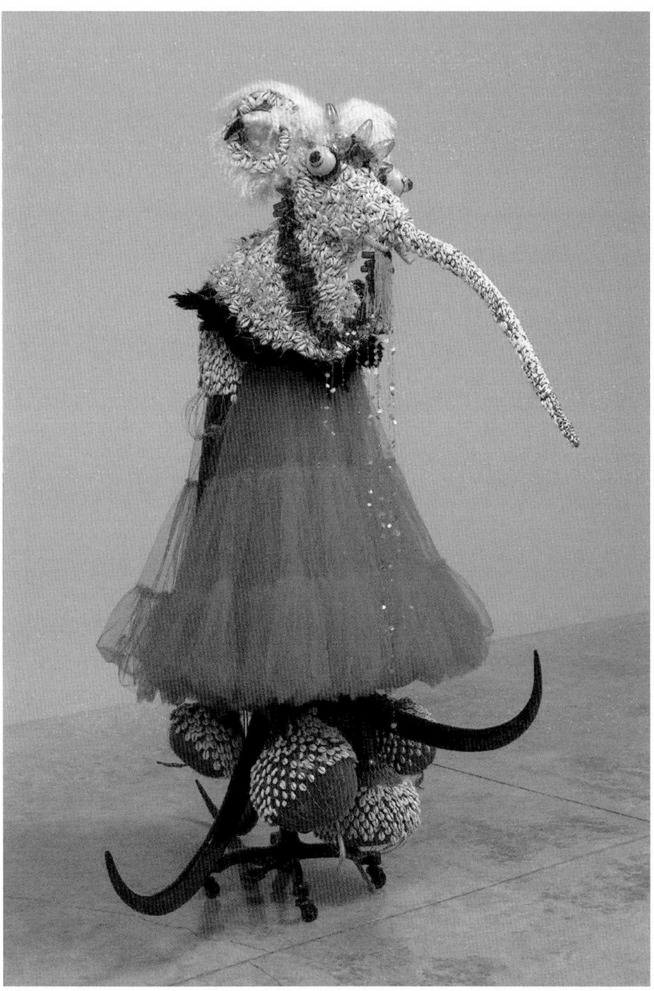

12 **Rina Banerjee**

She was now in western style dress covered in part of Empires' ruffle and red dress, had a foreign and peculiar race, a Ganesha who had lost her head, was thrown across sea until herself shipwrecked. A native of Bangladesh lost foot to root in Videsh, followed her mother full stop on forehead, trapped tongue of horn and grew ram-like under stress, 2011
cowrie shells, rooster feather, gourds, acrylic horns, ceramic balls, plastic netting, amber glass vials, violet glass bulbs, false glass doe, eyeballs, silk and synthetic Lanvin ruffled red dress; 73 x 65 inches
Collection of the National Taiwan Museum of Fine Arts, Taichung, Taiwan.

Afterword

Decolonizing Culture was born of the internet—a space where ideas feel more fluid and seem able to stretch across physical and social geographies that still, too often, get in our way. For those of us who exist on the margins of academic and art institutions, the internet is a tool that allows us to find one another, link arguments, dig up buried truths, empower words, be visible, and downright rabble-rouse when needed. We've built a community through it. The actual hashtags of the column from which these essays are pulled create an infinitely growing community and context that is immediately out of our control as publishers—a risky relay of thought and sharing that defines our new world of online information-building that is nonlinear and unstoppable. #Hashtags is more than a column—it has become a socio-political space, where words are power, stuffed into our own cannons, and shot across the desks of those who could easily ignore us.

I have thought a lot about what it means to take this column and turn it into one physical object that is fixed in time. In some ways it seems antithetical to pull #Hashtags from its online space—to pull one link from a growing online chainmail—and ask it to stand alone. Part of #Hashtags's success is how it connects to or is the connection between so many different people and organizations. But when I think about the context of this column, which exists in a world of Black Lives Matter, Donald Trump's election, and the relentless attack on the arts, I have come to learn that #Hashtags is a part of an exhausting and relentless criticality. It is part of a larger commitment to hold those in power and in the art world accountable while also supporting our communities.

When I joined *Daily Serving* and its sister publication *Art Practical*, one of my main goals was to develop our organization in a way that extended our institutional access in support of those who are historically not afforded it, in any way that we could. I am still determined. In this case, we are building a publishing imprint to not only create space for brilliant writers and thinkers but to also support these cultural workers on their own pathways to leadership and advancement. This is inclusive access-building and radical pedagogy—knowing that intersectional voices from our community will hold permanent physical space in a library, on a desk, and in a backpack, even after you close your web browser. As more of our higher education system relies on the inhumane labor of adjuncts, we see this book-publishing imprint as having an even greater purpose. The academic institution expects adjuncts to be brilliant professors, educators, mentors, and professionals in the field without institutional support—without basic employment necessities like job security, benefits, or living wages. This is particularly egregious knowing how much of this population identify as women of color and LGBTQI.

We hope that this text will be used as a pedagogical tool, whether for the classroom or for your own creative practice of learning. At the center of these essays is art and readings of artists through the worlds they are occupying. Art cannot be separated from the bodies that make it—the lives that those bodies live and inhabit. One's positionality—race, sexuality, gender, family narrative, religion, class, etc.—is no less a part of an artwork than themes like memory, attraction to a specific color palette, rising sea levels, or our society's increasing disconnect. So why do we keep insisting it is?

Like teaching, art is inherently of the body. Knowledge and information moves physically through us and is transmitted and translated through movement, voice, eye contact, and touch. Words are written on the board or typed into a computer. The thoughts that come from my brown fingers are offered to you—your body—to take in and contemplate. Thus we cannot separate the social impact of the body from how, who, what, and with what methods we teach. We cannot make those separations in how we read, view, and exchange artworks. To practice this is the radical pedagogy that we hope this book begins to create in your classroom. It is a reminder that we have much to learn and that change doesn't happen because we say it should. It is a reminder that the physical presence of women, practitioners of color, and LGBTQI-identified individuals and their dynamic ideas always belong with us, especially now.

Michele Carlson
Executive Director, *Daily Serving* and *Art Practical*
San Francisco, July 2017

Glossary

access — permission, liberty, or ability to enter, approach, or pass to and from a place or to approach or communicate with a person or thing. Freedom or ability to obtain or make use of something; a way or means of entering or approaching; in the context of education, access refers to students' equitable opportunities to take full advantage of resources made available to them.[1]

adjunct — a professor employed by a college or university for a specific purpose or length of time and often part-time.[2]

affective labor — the emotional dimension of service work; the invisible labor of emotional management most often performed by women and members of minority groups charged with the work of social reproduction within a system of commodity exchange.

appropriation — in the visual arts, appropriation is the intentional borrowing, copying, and alteration of preexisting images and objects.[3]

art collector — a person who collects works of art.[4]

art market — the art market, as distinct from art patronage, involves the sale (or resale) and distribution of works of art—including but not limited to antiquities, paintings, sculpture, tapestries, works on paper, ceramics, and metalwork—independent of direct commissions.[5]

beauty — the quality or aggregate of qualities in a person or thing that gives pleasure to the senses or pleasurably exalts the mind or spirit; a particularly graceful, ornamental, or excellent quality; a brilliant, extreme, or egregious example or instance; subject to aesthetic appreciation.[6]

capital — wealth in the form of money or assets, taken as a sign of the financial strength of an individual, organization, or nation, and assumed to be available for development or investment; money invested in a business to generate income; factors of production that are used to create goods or services and are not themselves in the process.[7]

class — a social stratum whose members share certain economic, social, or cultural characteristics: "the lower-income classes."[8]

collections — a group of objects gathered for study or exhibition; institutional collections can include archives, study or library collections, and object collections.[9]

conceptual art — art for which the idea (or concept) behind the work is more important than the finished art object. The term emerged to refer to an art movement in the 1960s and usually refers to art made from the mid-1960s to the mid-1970s.[10]

commerce — the exchange or buying and selling of commodities; especially the exchange of merchandise, on a large scale, between different places or communities; extended trade or traffic.[11]

creative economy — a creative economy is based on people's use of their creative imagination to increase an idea's value. John Howkins developed the concept in 2001 to describe economic systems where value is based on novel imaginative qualities rather than the traditional resources of land, labor, and capital; compared to creative industries, which are limited to specific sectors, the term is used to describe creativity throughout a whole economy. Some observers take the view that creativity is the defining characteristic of developed twenty-first century economies, just as manufacturing typified nineteenth and early twentieth centuries.[12]

cultural appropriation — cultural appropriation is the adoption or use of the elements of one culture by members of another culture; cultural appropriation, often framed as cultural misappropriation, is sometimes portrayed as harmful and is claimed to be a violation of the collective intellectual property rights of the originating culture.[13]

development — the process of economic and social transformation that is based on complex cultural and environmental factors and their interactions; the process of adding improvements to a parcel of land, such as grading, subdivisions, drainage, access, roads, utilities. Internally or externally generated investment in a region or community intended to generate economic or political activity.[14]

discrimination — the act, practice, or an instance of discriminating categorically rather than individually; prejudiced or prejudicial outlook, action, or treatment.[15]

displacement — the forced movement of people from their locality or environment and occupational activities, displacement is a form of social change caused by stress factors, the most common being armed conflict; natural disasters, famine, development, and economic changes may also be causes of displacement.[16]

embodiment — incarnation: to take a bodily form or become part of a body, incorporated; representation in human or animal form; personification.[17]

entrepreneur — person who organizes, operates, and assumes the risk for a business venture.[18]

ethnicity — an ethnic group; a social group that shares a common and distinctive culture, religion, language, or the like.[19]

fashion — the make or form of something; a mode of action or operation; a prevailing custom, usage, or style (as in dress); social standing or prominence especially as signalized by dress or conduct; the business of clothing design.[20]

gender — the behavioral, cultural, or psychological traits typically associated with one sex.[21]

gender expression — the expression of traits associated with gender, independent of their correlation with biologically determined sex and related social norms.

gentrification — the process of renewal and rebuilding accompanying the influx of middle class or affluent people into deteriorating areas that often displaces poorer residents;[22] the buying and renovation of houses and stores in deteriorated urban neighborhoods by upper- or middle-income families or individuals, raising property values but often displacing low-income families and small businesses.[23]

globalization — the transnational dimension of contemporary capitalism; globalization implies the opening of local and national markets and cultural sectors to an interconnected and interdependent global system of distributed capital investment, production, and consumption.

historicity — the historical actuality of persons and events, meaning the quality of being part of history as opposed to being a historical myth, legend, or fiction; historicity focuses on the true value of knowledge claims about the past (denoting historical actuality, authenticity, and factuality); the historicity of a claim about the past is its factual status.[24]

hybridity — popularized by Homi K. Bhabha, hybridity is the state of being at the border of two cultures, marked by a sense of "double consciousness" derived from the lexicon of Fanon and DuBois; hybridity is a subversion of single, unified, purist notions of identity, in favor of multiple cultural positions; Bhabha observes that, subsequent to cosmopolitanism and globalization, the hybrid migrant occupies a "third space" where the colonial and native identities meet and contest and are simultaneously asserted and subverted.[25]

industry — the manufacturing or technically productive enterprises in a particular field, country, region, or economy viewed collectively, or one of these individually; any general business activity or commercial enterprise that can be isolated from others, such as the tourist industry or the entertainment industry.[26]

intersectionality — intersectionality is a term coined by American civil rights lawyer Kimberlé Williams Crenshaw to describe overlapping or intersecting social identities and related systems of oppression, domination, or discrimination. Intersectional analysis recognizes that individuals often carry multiple overlapping identities that afford them varying degrees of power and make them vulnerable to specific instances of oppression; intersectional theory proposes that these intersecting identities ought to be viewed holistically rather than independently when addressing the causes and effects of structural discrimination on individuals.[27]

identity — the qualities, beliefs, personality, looks and/or expressions that make a person (self-identity) or group (particular social category or social group); the process of identity can be creative or destructive.[28]

institution — an establishment for the promotion of some object; an organized society or body of persons, usually with a fixed place of assemblage and operation, devoted to a special pursuit or purpose.[29]

institutional critique — an art term describing the systematic inquiry into the practices and ethos surrounding art institutions such as art academies, galleries, and museums, often challenging assumed and historical norms of artistic theory and practice; it often seeks to make visible the historically and socially constructed boundaries between inside and outside and public and private.[30]

labor — expenditure of physical or mental effort especially when difficult or compulsory; human activity that provides the goods or services in an economy; the services performed by workers for wages as distinguished from those rendered by entrepreneurs for profits.[31]

MFA — Master of Fine Arts; the terminal academic degree for collegiate faculty in Studio and Fine Art.

misogyny — hatred of, contempt for, or prejudice against women or girls; misogyny can be manifested in numerous ways, including social exclusion, sex discrimination, hostility, androcentrism, patriarchy, male privilege, belittling of women, violence against women, transphobia, and sexual objectification.[32]

museum — a building, place, or institution devoted to the acquisition, conservation, study, exhibition, and educational interpretation of objects having scientific, historical, or artistic value.[33]

nationalism — a range of political, social, and economic systems characterized by promoting the interests of a particular nation, particularly with the aim of gaining and maintaining self-governance, or full sovereignty, over the group's homeland; the political ideology therefore holds that a nation should govern itself, free from unwanted outside interference, and is linked to the concept of self-determination; nationalism is further oriented towards developing and maintaining a national identity based on shared characteristics such as culture, language, race, religion, political goals or a belief in a common ancestry.[34]

neocolonialism — the control of less-developed countries by developed countries through indirect means; the term neocolonialism was first used after World War II to refer to the continuing dependence of former colonies on foreign countries, but its meaning soon broadened to apply, more generally, to places where the power of developed countries was used to produce a colonial-like exploitation; the term is now an unambiguously negative one that is widely used to refer to a form of global power in which transnational corporations and global and multilateral institutions combine to perpetuate colonial forms of exploitation of developing countries; neocolonialism has been broadly theorized as a further development of capitalism that enables capitalist powers (both nations and corporations) to dominate subject nations through the operations of international capitalism rather than by means of direct rule.[35]

Orientalism — Orientalism is a term popularized by Edward Said used to describe the imitation or depiction of aspects of Middle Eastern, South Asian, and East Asian cultures in an idealized manner divorced from the lived experiences or political circumstances of the members of these communities; Orientalism is a form of soft power in which cultural appropriation and commerce drive the absorption and erasure of minority cultures.[36]

Other — a human being or group thereof, identified as outside the ontology of the self; an outsider; one who differs from the dominant social or cultural group; the condition of Otherness is a person's non-conformity to and with the social norms of society; and Otherness is the condition of disenfranchisement (political exclusion), effected either by the State or by the social institutions (e.g. the professions) invested with the corresponding socio-political power; the term Othering describes the reductive action of labelling a person as someone who belongs to a subordinate social category defined as the Other.[37]

painting — painting describes both the act of painting (using either a brush or other implement, such as palette knife, sponge, or airbrush to apply the paint); and the result of the action—the painting as an object.[38]

performance — the execution of an action; the fulfillment of a claim, promise, or request; the manner of reacting to stimuli; the linguistic behavior of an individual.[39]

performance art — in performance art, the artist's medium is the body, and the live actions of the performer are the work of art. Performance art usually consists of four elements: time, space, the performer's body, and a relationship between audience and performer; traditionally, the work is interdisciplinary, employing some other kind of visual art, video, sound, or props; many artists who initiated the genre in the 1960s performed their own work, but it is not a requirement of performance art that the artist participate in this manner.[40]

philanthropy — an idea, event, or action that is done to better humanity and usually involves some sacrifice as opposed to being done for a profit motive; acts of generosity.[41]

place — physical environment, physical surroundings; atmosphere; a proper or designated niche or setting; a site.[42]

postcolonialism — the historical period or state of affairs representing the aftermath of Western colonialism; the term can also be used to describe the concurrent project to reclaim and rethink the history and agency of people subordinated under various forms of imperialism; postcolonialism signals a possible future of overcoming colonialism, yet new forms of domination or subordination can come in the wake of such changes, including new forms of global empire; postcolonialism should not be confused with the claim that the world we live in now is actually devoid of colonialism.[43]

power — the ability to influence or control others through economic, political, social, or militaristic methods.

precarity — the politically induced condition in which certain populations suffer from failing social and economic networks of support and become differentially exposed to injury, violence, and death, at heightened risk of disease, poverty, starvation, displacement, and of exposure to violence without protection; precarity also characterizes that politically induced condition of maximized vulnerability and exposure for populations exposed to arbitrary state violence and to other forms of aggression that are not enacted by states and against which states do not offer adequate protection.[44]

protest — an individual or collective gesture or display of disapproval.[45]

punk — an ethos of independent cultural production manifested as music, art, and visual culture; punk integrates the popular aesthetics of rock music and avant-garde fashion with radical approaches to philosophy and political economy; "punk rock" usually refers to music recorded between 1976 and 1980 in the US, the UK, France, and Australia, but punk scenes have also emerged from non-Western cultures including Japan, Mexico, Brazil, and Indonesia.

race — a family, tribe, people, or nation belonging to the same stock; a class or kind of people unified by shared interests, habits, or characteristics; a category of humankind that shares certain distinctive physical traits.[46]

racism — the belief that a particular race is superior or inferior to another, and that a person's social and moral traits are predetermined by his or her inborn biological characteristics; racial separatism is the belief, most of the time based on racism, that different races should remain segregated and apart from one another.[47]

re-performance — to perform again or anew.[48]

representation — the act or action of representing; the state of being represented; the action or fact of one person standing for another so as to have the rights and obligations of the person represented;[49] the visual portrayal of someone or something;[50] cultural theorist Stuart Hall describes representation as the process by the process by which meaning is produced and exchanged between members of a culture through the use of language, signs, and images which stand for or represent things.[51]

rights — entitlements (not) to perform certain actions, or (not) to be in certain states; or entitlements that others (not) perform certain actions or (not) be in certain states; rights dominate modern understandings of what actions are permissible and which institutions are just; rights structure the form of governments, the content of laws, and the shape of morality as it is currently perceived.[52]

street art — visual art created in public locations; usually unsanctioned artwork executed outside of the context of traditional art venues; unlike traditional public art or monumental art, street art usually draws references from popular youth culture, commemorating the present and the ephemeral rather than the historically significant.[53]

style — a distinctive or characteristic manner of expression.[54]

support — to uphold by aid, encouragement, or countenance; to supply funds or means for; to assist in general; help; second; further; forward.[55]

technology — the practical application of science to commerce or industry.[56]

union — labor union: an organization of wage earners or salaried employees for mutual aid and protection and for dealing collectively with employers.[57]

violence — violence is the intentional use of physical force or power, threatened or actual, against oneself, another person, or against a group or community, which either results in or has a high likelihood of resulting in injury, death, psychological harm, maldevelopment, or deprivation.[58]

1   Amended from "access," *Merriam-Webster.com*, accessed August 15, 2017, https://www.merriam-webster.com/dictionary/access; and from "access," The Glossary of Education Reform, last modified March 10, 2014, http://edglossary.org/access/.

2   "adjunct professor," *Dictionary.com*, Random House, accessed August 15, 2017, http://www.dictionary.com/browse/adjunct-professor.

3   "Glossary of Art Terms," *MoMALearning*, accessed August 15, 2017, https://www.moma.org/learn/moma_learning/glossary.

4   "art collector," *Collins English Dictionary*, HarperCollins, accessed August 15, 2017, https://www.collinsdictionary.com/us/dictionary/english/art-collector.

5   "The Art Market and Collecting," *Encyclopedia.com*, accessed August 15, 2017, https://http://www.encyclopedia.com/history/encyclopedias-almanacs-transcripts-and-maps/art-market-and-collecting.

6   Amended from "beauty," *Merriam-Webster.com*, accessed August 15, 2017, https://https://www.merriam-webster.com/dictionary/beauty.

7   "capital," *BusinessDictionary*, WebFinance, accessed August 15, 2017, https://https://www.http://www.businessdictionary.com/definition/capital.html.

8   "class," *American Heritage Dictionary of the English Language*, Fifth Edition, Houghton Mifflin Harcourt, accessed August 15, 2017, https://ahdictionary.com/word/search.html?q=class.

9   Amended from "collection," *Merriam-Webster.com*, accessed August 15, 2017, https://www.merriam-webster.com/dictionary/collections.

10   "conceptual art," Art Terms, *Tate*, accessed August 15, 2017, http://www.tate.org.uk/art/art-terms/c/conceptual-art.

11   "commerce," *Wiktionary*, accessed August 15, 2017, https://en.wiktionary.org/wiki/commerce.

12   Amended from "creative economy (economic system)," *Wikipedia*, accessed August 15, 2017, https://en.wikipedia.org/wiki/Creative_economy_(economic_system).

13   "cultural appropriation," *Wikipedia*, accessed August 15, 2017, https://en.wikipedia.org/wiki/Cultural_appropriation.

14   "development," *BusinessDictionary*, WebFinance, accessed August 15, 2017, http://www.businessdictionary.com/definition/development.html.

15   Amended from "discrimination," *Merriam-Webster.com*, accessed August 15, 2017, https://www.merriam-webster.com/dictionary/discrimination.

16   Amended from "Displaced Person / Displacement," Social and Human Sciences: Themes, *UNESCO*, accessed August 15, 2017, http://www.unesco.org/new/en/social-and-human-sciences/themes/international-migration/glossary/displaced-person-displacement/.

17   Amended from "embody," *Merriam-Webster.com*, accessed August 15, 2017, https://www.merriam-webster.com/dictionary/embody.

18   "entrepreneur," *American Heritage Dictionary of the English Language*, Fifth Edition, Houghton Mifflin Harcourt, accessed August 15, 2017, https://ahdictionary.com/word/search.html?q=entrepreneur.

19 "ethnicity," *Dictionary.com*, Random House, accessed August 15, 2017, http://www.dictionary.com/browse/ethnicity.

20 Amended from "fashion," *Merriam-Webster.com*, accessed August 15, 2017, https://www.merriam-webster.com/dictionary/fashion.

21 Amended from "gender," *Merriam-Webster.com*, accessed August 15, 2017, https://www.merriam-webster.com/dictionary/gender.

22 "gentrification," *Merriam-Webster.com*, accessed August 15, 2017, https://www.merriam-webster.com/dictionary/gentrification.

23 "gentrification," *Dictionary.com*, Random House, accessed August 15, 2017, http://www.dictionary.com/browse/gentrification.

24 "historicity," *Wikipedia*, accessed August 15, 2017, https://en.wikipedia.org/wiki/Historicity.

25 Amended from Nasrullah Mambrol, "Homi Bhabha's Concept of Hybridity," *Literariness* (blog), accessed August 15, 2017, https://literariness.wordpress.com/2016/04/08/homi-bhabhas-concept-of-hybridity/.

26 Amended from "industry," *BusinessDictionary*, WebFinance, accessed August 15, 2017, http://www.businessdictionary.com/definition/industry.html.

27 Amended from "intersectionality," *Wikipedia*, accessed August 15, 2017, https://en.wikipedia.org/wiki/Intersectionality.

28 "identity (social science)," *Wikipedia*, accessed August 15, 2017, https://en.wikipedia.org/wiki/Identity_(social_science).

29 "institution," *The Century Dictionary and Cyclopedia*, accessed August 15, 2017, http://www.wordnik.com/words/institution.

30 "Glossary of Art Terms," *MoMALearning*.

31 Amended from "labor," *Merriam-Webster.com*, accessed August 15, 2017, https://www.merriam-webster.com/dictionary/labor.

32 Amended from "misogyny," *Wikipedia*, accessed August 15, 2017, https://en.wikipedia.org/wiki/Misogyny.

33 "museum," *American Heritage Dictionary of the English Language*, Fifth Edition, Houghton Mifflin Harcourt, accessed August 15, 2017, https://ahdictionary.com/word/search.html?q=museum.

34 "nationalism," *Wikipedia*, accessed August 15, 2017, https://en.wikipedia.org/wiki/Nationalism.

35 Amended from Sandra Halperin, "Neocolonialism," *Encyclopædia Britannica*, accessed August 15, 2017, https://www.britannica.com/topic/neocolonialism

36 Amended from "Orientalism," *Wikipedia*, accessed August 15, 2017, https://en.wikipedia.org/wiki/Orientalism.

37 Amended from "Other (philosophy)," *Wikipedia*, accessed August 15, 2017, https://en.wikipedia.org/wiki/Other_(philosophy).

38 Amended from "painting," Art Terms, *Tate*, accessed August 15, 2017, http://www.tate.org.uk/art/art-terms/p/painting.

39 Amended from "performance," *Merriam-Webster.com*, accessed August 15, 2017, https://www.merriam-webster.com/dictionary/performance.

40   Amended from "Performance into Art," *MoMALearning*, accessed August 15, 2017, https://www.moma.org/learn/moma_learning/themes/conceptual-art/performance-into-art.

41   Amended from "philanthropy," *BusinessDictionary*, WebFinance, accessed August 15, 2017, http://www.businessdictionary.com/definition/philanthropy.html.

42   Amended from "place," *Merriam-Webster.com*, accessed August 15, 2017, https://www.merriam-webster.com/dictionary/place.

43   Amended from Duncan Ivison, "Neocolonialism," *Encyclopædia Britannica*, accessed August 15, 2017, https://www.britannica.com/event/postcolonialism.

44   Amended from Judith Butler, "Performativity, Precariety and Sexual Politics," *AIBR* 4 No. 3, http://www.aibr.org/antropologia/04v03/criticos/040301b.pdf.

45   "protest," *American Heritage Dictionary of the English Language*, Fifth Edition, Houghton Mifflin Harcourt, accessed August 15, 2017, https://ahdictionary.com/word/search.html?q=protest.

46   Amended from "race," *Merriam-Webster.com*, accessed August 15, 2017, https://www.merriam-webster.com/dictionary/race.

47   "racism," *Anti-Defamation League*, accessed August 15, 2017, https://www.adl.org/racism.

48   "reperformance," *Wikipedia*, accessed August 15, 2017, https://en.wiktionary.org/wiki/reperformance.

49   Amended from "representation," *Merriam-Webster.com*, accessed August 15, 2017, https://www.merriam-webster.com/dictionary/representation.

50   "Glossary of Art Terms," *MoMALearning*.

51   Alisa Acosta, "Representation, meaning, and language," *Alisa Acosta* (blog), accessed August 15, 2017, http://ohmissacosta.com/blog/representation-meaning-and-language/.

52   Amended from "rights," *Stanford Encyclopedia of Philosophy*, accessed August 15, 2017, https://plato.stanford.edu/entries/rights/.

53   Amended from "street art," *Wikipedia*, accessed August 15, 2017, https://en.wikipedia.org/wiki/Street_art.

54   "Glossary of Art Terms," *MoMALearning*.

55   "support," *The Century Dictionary and Cyclopedia*, accessed August 15, 2017, http://www.wordnik.com/words/support.

56   "technology," from *WordNet* 3.0, Princeton University, 2006, http://www.wordnik.com/words/technology.

57   "labor union," *Dictionary.com*, Random House, accessed August 15, 2017, http://www.dictionary.com/browse/labor-union.

58   "violence," *World Health Organization*, acessed August 15, 2017, http://www.who.int/topics/violence/en/.

Bilbliography

Ahmed, Sara. "Declarations of Whiteness: The Non-Performativity of Anti-Racism." *Borderlands e-journal* 3, no. 2 (2004). http://www.borderlands.net.au/vol3no2_2004/ahmed_declarations.htm.

Ahmed, Sara. *The Cultural Politics of Emotion.* New York: Routledge, 2004.

Allan, Scott C. "Interrogating Gustave Moreau's Sphinx: Myth as Artistic Metaphor in the 1864 Salon." *Nineteenth Century Art Worldwide* 7, no. 1, 2008. http://www.19thc-artworldwide.org/spring08/39-spring08/spring08article/110-interrogating-gusave-moreaus-sphinx-myth-as-artistic-metaphor-at-the-1864-salon.

Amadasun, David Osa. "'Black People Don't Go to Galleries'—The reproduction of taste and cultural value." *Media Diversified,* October 21, 2013. https://mediadiversified.org/2013/10/21/black-people-dont-go-to-galleries-the-reproduction-of-taste-and-cultural-value/.

Appiah, Kwame Anthony. *Cosmopolitanism: Ethics in a World of Strangers.* New York and London: WW Norton and Company, 2006.

Artforum. "Director of Contemporary Art Museum St. Louis Responds to Critics of Decision to Wall Off Kelley Walker Exhibition." October 12, 2016. https://www.artforum.com/news/id=64013.

Bhabha, Homi. *The Location of Culture.* London and New York: Routledge, 2004.

Berger, Martin. *Seeing through Race: A Reinterpretation of Civil Rights Photography.* Berkeley: UC Press, 2011.

Boucher, Brian. "Dana Schutz Responds to the Uproar Over Her Emmett Till Painting at the Whitney Biennial." *artnet,* March 23, 2017. https://news.artnet.com/art-world/dana-schutz-responds-to-the-uproar-over-her-emmett-till-painting-900674.

Carrico, Dale. "San Francisco Art Institute Touts Diego Rivera Fresco Celebrating Labor Politics While Engaging in Union Busting." *Amor Mundi* (blog), May 1, 2014. https://amormundi.blogspot.com/2014/05/san-francisco-art-institute-touts-diego.html.

Center for the Future of Museums. *Demographic Transformation and the Future of Museums.* Washington DC: American Association of Museums Press, 2010. http://www.aam-us.org/docs/center-for-the-future-of-museums/demotransaam2010.pdf

Charlesworth, JJ. "Playing Politics: JJ Charlesworth on Why Art World Hypocrisy Stars at the 56th Venice Biennale." *artnet,* May 7, 2015. https://news.artnet.com/art-world/56th-venice-biennale-politics-jj-charlesworth-295350.

Davis, Ben. *9.5 Theses on Art and Class.* New York: Haymarket Books, 2013.

Deleuze, Gilles, and Félix Guattari. *A Thousand Plateaus.* London and New York: Bloomsbury Academic, 2013.

Del Pesco, Joseph and Bean Gilsdorf. "What's up with stARTup?" *Open Space,* January 28, 2015. http://openspace.sfmoma.org/2015/01/whats-up-with-startup/.

DiAngelo, Robin. "White Fragility: Why It's So Hard to Talk to White People About Racism." *The Good Men Project,* April 9, 2015. https://goodmenproject.com/featured-content/white-fragility-why-its-so-hard-to-talk-to-white-people-about-racism-twlm/.

Díaz, Junot. "MFA vs. POC." *New Yorker*, April 30, 2014. http://www.newyorker.com/books/page-turner/mfa-vs-poc.

Duray, Dan. "Stefan Simchowitz vs. the Art World." *Observer*, May 7, 2014. http://observer.com/2014/05/stefan-simchowitz-vs-the-art-world/.

Fanon, Frantz. *Black Skin, White Masks*, translated by Charles Lam Markham. New York: Grove Press, 1967.

Frey, Raman. "Art and Tech in the Bay Area: Better Together." *Medium* (blog), January 19, 2014. https://medium.com/@ramanfrey/art-and-tech-in-the-bay-area-e503f3f3601e.

Glazek, Christopher. "The Art World's Patron Satan." *New York Times Magazine*, December 30, 2014. https://www.nytimes.com/2015/01/04/magazine/the-art-worlds-patron-satan.html.

Glissant, Édouard. *Poetics of Relation*, translated by Betsy Wing. Ann Arbor, MI: University of Michigan Press, 1997.

Goldstein, Andrew. "Why Dana Schutz's Emmett Till Painting Must Stay: A Q&A With the Whitney Biennial's Christopher Lew." *artnet*, March 30, 2017. https://news.artnet.com/art-world/whitney-biennial-christopher-lew-dana-schutz-906557.

Greenberger, Alex. "'The Painting Must Go': Hannah Black Pens Open Letter to the Whitney About Controversial Biennial Work." *ARTnews*, March 21, 2017. http://www.artnews.com/2017/03/21/the-painting-must-go-hannah-black-pens-open-letter-to-the-whitney-about-controversial-biennial-work/.

Grynbaum, Michael M. "De Blasio Brings Hope for a Populist Arts Revival." *New York Times*, December 29, 2013. http://www.nytimes.com/2013/12/30/arts/a-new-mayor-brings-hope-for-a-populist-arts-revival.html.

Hall, Stuart, Jessica Evans, and Sean Nixon, eds. *Representation*, second edition. Los Angeles: Sage; Milton Keynes, UK: The Open University, 2013.

Heddaya, Mostafa. "Artist Collective Withdraws from Whitney Biennial [UPDATED]." *Hyperallergic*, May 14, 2014. https://hyperallergic.com/126420/artist-collective-withdraws-from-whitney-biennial/.

Higgins, Charlotte. "Das Kapital at the Arsenale: How Okwui Enwezor Invited Marx to the Biennale." *Guardian*, May 7, 2015. http://www.theguardian.com/artanddesign/2015/may/07/das-kapital-at-venice-biennale-okwui-enwezor-karl-marx.

hooks, bell. "An Aesthetic of Blackness: Strange and Oppositional." *Lenox Avenue: A Journal of Interarts Inquiry* 1 (1995).

Johnson, Rin. "On Hearing a White Man Co-opt the Body of Michael Brown." *Hyperallergic*, March 20, 2015. https://hyperallergic.com/192628/on-hearing-a-white-man-co-opt-the-body-of-michael-brown/.

Jordan, Marvin. "Hito Steyerl: Politics of Post-Representation." *dis magazine*, n.d. http://dismagazine.com/disillusioned-2/62143/hito-steyerl-politics-of-post-representation/.

Kennedy, Randy. "White Artist's Painting of Emmett Till at Whitney Biennial Draws Protests." *New York Times*, March 21, 2017. https://www.nytimes.com/2017/03/21/arts/design/painting-of-emmett-till-at-whitney-biennial-draws-protests.html.

King, Jamilah. "Kara Walker's Sugar Sphinx Evokes Call From Black Women: 'We Are Here.'" *Colorlines*, June 23, 2014. http://www.colorlines.com/articles/kara-walkers-sugar-sphinx-evokes-call-black-women-we-are-here.

Lacy, Suzanne. *Mapping the Terrain: New Genre Public Art*. Seattle: Bay Press, 1995.

Leefeb, Felicia R. "Singular Art, Made by Plurals: Yams Collective Brings Work to Whitney Biennial." *New York Times*, February 21, 2014. https://www.nytimes.com/2014/02/22/arts/design/yams-collective-brings-work-to-whitney-biennial.html.

Los Angeles County Economic Development Corporation. *2014 Otis Report on the Creative Economy*, April 2015. https://www.otis.edu/sites/default/files/2015_Otis_Report_on_the_Creative_Economy_CA.pdf.

Mack, Heather. "Royalty of the Mission Art Scene Faces Eviction." *Mission Local*, October 2, 2013. http://missionlocal.org/2013/10/royalty-of-the-mission-art-scene-faces-eviction/.

Markusen, Ann, and Anne Gadwa. *Creative Placemaking*, white paper for the Mayors' Institute on City Design, 2010. https://www.arts.gov/sites/default/files/CreativePlacemaking-Paper.pdf.

Mathur, Saloni, ed. *The Migrant's Time: Rethinking Art History and Diaspora*. Williamstown, MA: Sterling and Francine Clark Institute; New Haven, CT: Distributed by Yale University Press, 2011.

McAnally, James. "A Call for a Collective Reexamination of Our Art Institutions." *Hyperallergic*, October 11, 2016. https://hyperallergic.com/329506/call-collective-reexamination-art-institutions/.

McEvilley, Thomas. *The Triumph of Anti-Art*. Kingston, New York: McPherson & Co., 2005.

Moraga, Cherrie and Gloria Anzaldua, eds. *This Bridge Called My Back: Writings by Radical Women of Color*. Watertown, MA: Persephone Press, 1981.

Morse, Jack. "Report: Ellis Act Filings Up 36% As Evictions Hit Six-Year High." *SFist*, March 29, 2016. http://sfist.com/2016/03/29/report_evictions_continue_to_increa.php.

Muñoz-Alonso, Lorena. "Why Does Vik Muniz's Giant Paper Boat for the Venice Biennale Trivialize Europe's Migrant Crisis?" *artnet*, April 22, 2015. https://news.artnet.com/exhibitions/vik-muniz-paper-boat-venice-biennale-290752.

Parenti, Michael. *Dirty Truths*. San Francisco: City Lights Books: 1996.

Purves, Ted and Shane Aslan Selzer. *What We Want is Free*, second edition. Albany: SUNY Press, 2014.

Saltz, Jerry. "Saltz on Stefan Simchowitz, the Greatest Art-Flipper of Them All." *Vulture*, March 31, 2014. http://www.vulture.com/2014/03/saltz-on-the-great-and-powerful-simchowitz.html.

Segran, Elizabeth. "The Adjunct Revolt: How Poor Professors Are Fighting Back." *Atlantic*, April 28, 2014. https://www.theatlantic.com/business/archive/2014/04/the-adjunct-professor-crisis/361336/.

Smith, Terry. *Contemporary Art: World Currents*. Upper Saddle River, New Jersey: Pearson Education, 2011.

Solnit, Rebecca. Diary. *London Review of Books* 35, no. 3, February 7, 2013. https://www.lrb.co.uk/v35/n03/rebecca-solnit/diary.

Solnit, Rebecca. "Welcome to the (Don't Be) Evil Empire: Google Eats the World." *TomDispatch*, June 25, 2013. http://www.tomdispatch.com/blog/175717/tomgram%3A_rebecca_solnit%2C_how_to_act_like_a_billionaire.

Spivak, Gayatri Chakravorty. *A Critique of Postcolonial Reason: Toward a History of the Vanishing Present.* Cambridge, MA: Harvard University Press, 1999.

Steinhauer, Jillian. "The Depressing Stats of the 2014 Whitney Biennial." *Hyperallergic*, November 15, 2013. https://hyperallergic.com/93821/the-depressing-stats-of-the-2014-whitney-biennial/.

Steyerl, Hito, and Marvin Jordan. "Hito Steyerl, Politics of Post-Representation." In conversation, *dis magazine*, n.d. http://dismagazine.com/disillusioned-2/62143/hito-steyerl-politics-of-post-representation/.

Swanson, Carl. "How Oscar Murillo Perfectly Encapsulates the Current State of the Contemporary Art World." *Vulture*, July 3, 2014. http://www.vulture.com/2014/06/oscar-murillo-perfectly-represents-contemporary-art-world.html.

Vartanian, Hrag. "Artist Walid Raad Denied Entry into UAE, Becoming Third Gulf Labor Member Turned Away." *Hyperallergic*, May 14, 2015. http://hyperallergic.com/207176/artist-walid-raad-denied-entry-into-uae-becoming-third-gulf-labor-member-turned-away/.

Walker, Kara, and Kara Rooney. "A Sonorous Subtlety: Kara Walker with Kara Rooney." In Conversation, *The Brooklyn Rail*, May 6, 2014. http://brooklynrail.org/2014/05/art/kara-walker-with-kara-rooney.

Whitney Museum of American Art, "Donelle Woolford: Dick's Last Stand at The Kitchen, New York | Whitney Museum of American Art," http://whitney.org/Exhibitions/2014Biennial/DonelleWoolford.

Index

Acknowledgements

Special thanks to my partner Stephan Bugaj, my editor Bean Gilsdorf, and my parents, Revathi and Bhadrasain Vikram, for your care, support, and grounding perspectives.

This book would not have been possible without the time and labor of the women and men who prepare my family's food, clean my house, teach and care for my children, and otherwise make it possible for me to write. You have my deepest thanks.

Author Bio

Anuradha Vikram is a writer, curator, and educator based in Los Angeles. She is the artistic director at 18th Street Arts Center in Santa Monica, California. Her research combines media studies, theory of globalization, and critical race discourse with early modern, modern, and contemporary art history. Publications include "'Naked in the Sight of the Object': Masking, Masquerade, and Black Identity" (*X-TRA*, vol. 18 no. 4, Summer 2016), "Becoming Human: Nam June Paik's Futuristic Compassion" (*X-TRA*, vol. 18 no. 1, Fall 2015), "A Brief and Incomplete History of Art and Technology Ventures in the Bay Area 1980–2010" (*Afterimage*, vol. 41, no. 6, Summer 2014), and "Sonya Rapoport: A Woman's Place is in the Studio" (*Sonya Rapoport: Pairings of Polarities*. Berkeley: Heyday, 2012). She has contributed to *Leonardo*, *KCET Artbound*, *Artillery*, *Hyperallergic*, *Daily Serving*, and *OPEN SPACE*, the blog of the San Francisco Museum of Modern Art. She is a Senior Lecturer at Otis College of Art and Design, and a member of the Board of Directors of the College Art Association, where she serves on the Conference committee and chairs the Museums committee.

Decolonizing Culture:
Essays on the Intersection of Art and Politics
Anuradha Vikram

Editor
Bean Gilsdorf

Copy Editor
Victoria Gannon

Proofreaders
Addy Rabinovitch
Charmaine Koh

Design
Sming Sming Books

Publishers
ART PRACTICAL BOOKS
Sming Sming Books

Art Practical
Executive Director
Michele Carlson

Editor in Chief
Kara Q. Smith

Operations Manager
Addy Rabinovitch

Communications Manager
Eden Redmond

First Edition
Printed in Santa Clara, CA

Art Practical
California College of the Arts
1111 8th Street
San Francisco, CA

ISBN 978-0-9985006-5-2